THE STORY OF THE WORLD

BOOK I.

ON THE SHORES OF THE GREAT SEA

*FROM THE DAYS OF ABRAHAM TO
THE BIRTH OF CHRIST*

THE RETURN OF ULYSSES

ON THE SHORES OF THE GREAT SEA

BY

M. B. SYNGE

ILLUSTRATED BY E. M. SYNGE, A.R.E.

YESTERDAY'S CLASSICS

CHAPEL HILL, NORTH CAROLINA

This edition, first published in 2006 by Yesterday's Classics, is an unabridged republication of the work originally published by William Blackwood and Sons in 1903. For a listing of books published by Yesterday's Classics, please visit www.yesterdaysclassics.com. Yesterday's Classics is the publishing arm of the Baldwin Project which presents the complete text of dozens of classic books for children at www.mainlesson.com under the editorship of Lisa M. Ripperton and T. A. Roth.

ISBN-10:   1-59915-013-1

ISBN-13:   978-1-59915-013-0

Yesterday's Classics
PO Box 3418
Chapel Hill, NC 27515

CONTENTS

Page

CHAPTER 1

THE HOME OF ABRAHAM

"In the faith of little children, we went on our ways."
—KIPLING.

IT is strange to think of a very old world, when men knew nothing of the great salt sea that washed their shores, and nothing of the wonderful lands, that lay beyond. Each day the sun rose and set as it does to-day, but they did not know the reason why: the rivers flowed through the land, but they did not know whence they came, or whither they went.

These men of old, knew one great fact. They knew that they must live in a land, where there was plenty of water. How else could their sheep and oxen stay their thirst? how else should they and their children get food and drink? and how should the grain grow to save the land from famine?

So wherever a man settled down with his family in the old days, he chose some place near a river or spring. Perhaps others would wander over the land till they came to the same river, and there they would settle too, until there would be quite a little colony of families all attracted to the same spot

1

by the fact that fresh, clean water, was flowing through the land.

And so it was that, long ago, the old stories tell us of a group of men, women, and children, who came and settled around a great river, called the Euphrates, away in the far East. It was one of the four rivers that watered the garden of Eden—a very beautiful and fertile spot.

This little group of settlers—known as the Chaldeans—grew corn in their rich country and became very prosperous, while other men were wandering about the trackless land with no fixed abode or calling.

These Chaldeans taught themselves many things. They made bricks and built houses to live in, they looked at the deep blue sky over their heads and learnt about the sun; they wandered about by night and learnt about the moon and the stars, they divided their time into seven days and called the days after seven stars, they taught themselves arithmetic and geometry. Of course they had no paper and pens to write with, but they scratched simple pictures on stones and tablets. For instance, a little drawing of one nail meant the figure I., two nails meant II., three nails in a row meant III., and so on.

Even to-day men go out to this old country, which has long since ceased to take any part in the world's history, and they find the old stones and tablets scratched by the Chaldeans, and learn more about these industrious people.

The Chaldeans knew a great deal, but they knew nothing beyond their own country, for how should they? There were no carts, no trains, no bridges over the rivers, no ships, in those early days. Travelling was very slow and difficult. On the backs of camels or asses the journeys must be made, under the burning sun and over the trackless desert land: food must be carted, and even water; for how could they tell where rivers ran in those unknown, unexplored regions?

But the day was at hand when one man with his whole family should travel from this land beyond the Euphrates, travel away from the busy life of the Chaldean cities into a new and unknown country.

That man was known as Abraham.

He was a great man in the far East; he was well read in the stars, and had learnt much about the rising and setting of the sun and moon. Why he was called to leave his native land is not known. "Get thee out of thine own country, and from thy kindred, and from thy father's house, unto a land that I will show thee."

These were Abraham's orders.

And one day he rose up, and taking his old father Terah, his wife Sarai, and his fatherless young nephew Lot, with camels and asses bearing all his possessions, he left Chaldea.

The little party journeyed for a day, perhaps more, until they came to the frontier fortress of their own country, and here the old father Terah died

3

before ever he had crossed that river that bounded the land of his birth.

And Abraham started off again to travel into the unknown land. The great river Euphrates rolled its vast volume of waters between him and the country to which his steps were bent. Two days' journey would bring him to the high chalk cliffs, from which he could overlook the wide western desert. Broad and strong lay the great stream below. He crossed it, probably near the same point where it is still forded. He crossed it and became known as the Hebrew—the man who had crossed the river flood—the man who came from beyond the Euphrates.

CHAPTER 2

INTO AFRICA

"And Abraham went down into Egypt to sojourn there."
—GEN. xii. 10.

THE land of Canaan was now before him. It was a low-lying country, now marked on modern maps as Syria,—the old highway between the tract of land known as Asia and that known now as Africa. Its coast was washed by the blue sea, known to men of old time as the Great Sea, on the waters of which no one had as yet ventured to trust themselves.

As pilgrims travel now in the East, so would Abraham have travelled then through this land of Canaan, with his wife and young Lot. With all his possessions heaped high on the backs of camels and asses, with his slaves running along by his side, with his flocks of sheep and goats moving under the towering forms of the camels, he would start slowly into the new country. Abraham himself, in a scarlet robe, as chief of the tribe, would guide the march, settling where the nightly tent should be pitched, and arranging pasture and water for the flocks and herds. On and on, under the fiercely blazing sun, the long caravan would slowly travel, ever journeying southwards.

He was the first explorer of a new land of whom there is a full account.

But while he yet journeyed, there came on one of those droughts to which the land of Canaan was always subject, when day after day the sky was blue and cloudless, when no rains fell to water the thirsty land, and Abraham went on still farther south till he reached Africa.

Now, while the great colony on the banks of the river Euphrates was growing and thriving away in Asia, another colony was growing along the banks of the Nile—the greatest river in Africa. Here family after family had come, attracted by the fertile land watered by the Nile, in just the same way as the Chaldeans had settled by the Euphrates. And this country was known as Egypt—the gift of the Nile.

So out of the shadowland of early history we get these two settlements—the Chaldeans on the Euphrates in Asia and the Egyptians on the Nile in Africa. They were hundreds of miles apart, and though men may have journeyed from one to the other before, yet Abraham is the first traveller of whom we have any record.

It must have been with feelings of awe that he approached the land of Egypt. He might be denied the corn he had come hither to obtain, he might be slain, unknown dangers and difficulties might lie before him. He must have been surprised at what he found in Egypt, after all. He found a very old settlement, as old as—perhaps older than—that from which he had come.

The Egyptians could tell him stories of a king, that had ruled over them thousands of years ago, called Menes, a king

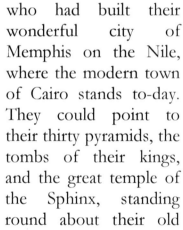

who had built their wonderful city of Memphis on the Nile, where the modern town of Cairo stands to-day. They could point to their thirty pyramids, the tombs of their kings, and the great temple of the Sphinx, standing round about their old city, even as some of them stand round about Cairo to-day.

They could tell Abraham the story of how those pyramids were built; of the immense granite blocks which were brought five hundred miles; of the great causeway, which took ten years to construct, along which these blocks could be carried; of the twenty years it took to build one pyramid, and

7

the thousands and thousands of men employed in the work.

And under these massive structures the old Eastern kings slept their last sleep; while to-day we still wonder at the industry and patience of the ancient Egyptians.

"Soldiers," said the great Napoleon, as he led the French army through the heart of Egypt some hundred years ago—"Soldiers, forty centuries look down upon you, from the top of the pyramids."

Indeed, later on, when roads cut up the countries of the earth, and ships sailed on the seas, these old pyramids of Egypt were ranked among the Seven Wonders of the World.

This strange land to which Abraham had come was a land of plenty; there was corn growing along the fertile valley, for the mighty Nile depended not on local rains to water the earth. And the great king, or Pharaoh, as he was called, treated Abraham well. It is said that the Chaldean explorer taught the Egyptians astronomy; he certainly did well in the strange land, and when he left, Pharaoh gave him sheep and oxen, men-servants and maid-servants, and Abraham was a very rich man.

CHAPTER 3

AN OLD TRADE-ROUTE

"Then there passed by . . . merchantmen."
—GEN. xxxvii. 28.

IT was a much larger caravan which passed out of
Egypt, when the time came at last for Abraham to
go back to Canaan; there were more flocks and
herds, sheep and cattle, camels and asses. They
returned by the same way they came, till they
reached one of their old camping-grounds near
Bethel.

But Abraham and Lot were no longer
wandering explorers, in search of pasture for their
flocks. They were rich men now, with numerous
attendants, and the pasture that was enough to feed
all, in the old days, was no longer enough for both.
And there was some quarrelling between the
herdmen of Abraham's cattle and the herdmen of
Lot's cattle.

Together, the two men stood on a piece of
rising ground, from which they could look over the
surrounding country.

"Is not the whole land before thee?" said the older man, who had already made up his mind as to the future. "Separate thyself, I pray thee, from me; if thou wilt take the left hand, then I will go to the right; or if thou depart to the right hand, then I will go to the left."

And Lot, knowing the value of the river Jordan which flowed through the midst of the land, chose its fertile plain, which was well watered everywhere, like the land of Egypt, from which he had just come. So he took his servants, his cattle, and his sheep, and there he made his new home.

Abraham lived in Canaan, right away from Lot; but he did not forget the little colony that had settled in the plains of Jordan—like a branch from the old root,—and when Lot was in difficulties with his foes, Abraham was the first to go to his help.

It was the same in those old days as it is now; the mother country helps her colonies, when they are in trouble.

After a time Abraham's descendants possessed the whole land of Canaan, which reached from his old home beyond the river Euphrates to the river Nile in Egypt. But the love of the old country was still strong within him; and when it was time to choose a wife for his son Isaac, it was to the land beyond the Euphrates that he turned.

Thence came Rebekah, who became the grandmother of Joseph, the story of whose life in Egypt is at once so pathetic and interesting.

As time went on, there was more and more traffic between the two settlements in Asia and Africa, through the land of Canaan. More than one route was discovered by which the long lines of camels and caravans could pass with safety from the one country to the other. And why should they want to go from one land to the other? For purposes of trade.

If one settlement could make and produce what another settlement could not, it was natural that an exchange should take place. And so it came to pass that long lines of camels were constantly journeying across Canaan bearing spices, balm, and myrrh into Egypt, and taking back with them silk and ivory from that country. It was to one of these parties of merchantmen, that Joseph was sold— merchants, on their way down into Egypt.

The story of Joseph is familiar to every child. They know how he was loved by his father Jacob, and how he lived with his parents in the land of Canaan, inherited from his grandfather Abraham. How his elder brothers had gone south to pasture their flocks, like the Arabs of the present day, wherever the wild country was unowned. How by-and-by Jacob, growing uneasy about his elder sons, sent Joseph,—then a boy of seventeen,—clad in his coat of many colours, to see how they were getting on. How the elder brothers hated Joseph because he was his father's favourite, and how, when they saw him coming, they whispered among themselves, "Come now, therefore, and let us slay him."

11

Finally, they sold him to the party of merchants passing with their camels, laden with spices, for Egypt. So the boy Joseph, now robbed of his coat of many colours, was carried off to Egypt, and there sold to one Potiphar, a courtier of the great Pharaoh of the country.

And while Joseph was serving in Egypt his old father was weeping for him away in Canaan.

"All his sons and all his daughters rose up to comfort him; but he refused to be comforted."

Little did Jacob think, as he mourned for Joseph as dead, that some day he too should travel down to Egypt, where he should find his son again, "governor over all the land."

CHAPTER 4

JOSEPH IN EGYPT

"Governor over all the land of Egypt."
—GEN. xlv. 26.

THERE had been changes in Egypt since the days of Abraham. The long line of native kings had come to an end, and some new rulers or Pharaohs had arisen, known as "Shepherd kings." It was during the reign of one of these shepherd kings that Joseph was sold into Egypt. There had been a great deal of fighting, too, in the country, and now the tract of land belonging to the Egyptians was much larger than of old, and a wonderful new city called Thebes had been built on the Nile, some distance above Memphis.

Now these Pharaohs ruling over Egypt were held to be very great men, and they were treated with great pomp and dignity. The old tablets and monuments tell us, in their quaint picture stories, how splendid were the courts of these kings, and how all men bowed down to them. They tell us stories of the king's household: of his many servants, the royal barbers and perfumers, shoemakers, tailors;

13

of those who presided over the royal linen, of the laundresses who washed it in the river Nile. They tell us of the troops of musicians, singers, dancers, cooks, butlers, bakers, and magicians.

The Egyptians of old drew pictures showing how the Pharaohs received taxes from the people, not in money, for they did not use money in those days, but in fruit, oxen, or grain. And there were buildings connected with the royal palace at Memphis: there was the storehouse for grain, the storehouse for fruit, and the white storehouse, where stuffs and jewels are kept.

So the Pharaohs were very rich and powerful, and they did as they pleased with their kingdoms. Joseph would have heard all about the ruler of Egypt from his master, but being a slave himself he would have had no chance of seeing him.

Now, since he had been in Egypt, Joseph had shown himself very clever at explaining dreams, and this fact came to the ears of the great Pharaoh, who was puzzling sorely over a strange dream he had lately had.

So he sent for the young Hebrew servant, and Joseph stood before Pharaoh.

"I have dreamed a dream," said the great king, "and there is none that can interpret it: and I have heard say of thee, that thou canst understand a dream to interpret it."

It must have been a great moment for the young stranger from Canaan as he listened to

Joseph before Pharaoh

Pharaoh's dream, but his fame had not gone abroad in vain. He understood the dream, and he said to Pharaoh:

"Behold, there come seven years of great plenty throughout all the land of Egypt: and there shall arise after them seven years of famine; and all the plenty shall be forgotten in the land of Egypt; and the famine shall consume the land; and the plenty shall not be known in the land by reason of that famine following; for it shall be very grievous."

Then, unbidden, Joseph went on to tell the king what had better be done to save the land.

"Let Pharaoh look out a man discreet and wise, and set him over the land of Egypt. . . And let him appoint officers over the land, and take up the fifth part of the land of Egypt in the seven plenteous years. And let them gather all the food of those good years that come, and lay up corn under the hand of Pharaoh, and let them keep food in the cities. . . That the land perish not through the famine."

The words of the young stranger showed great foresight, at which the king must have marvelled. Surely such wisdom was no common thing.

"Can we find such a one as this is?" he said to his servants round him. Then turning to Joseph he said:

"Thou shalt be over my house, and according unto thy word shall all my people be ruled: only in the throne will I be greater than thou. . . See, I have set thee over all the land of Egypt."

And so, while his father mourned for him as dead in the land of Canaan, Joseph was governor over all the land of Egypt—second only to the king. Instead of the little coat of many colours, he now wore the white robe of state, the king's own ring was on his finger, the king's own gold chain was about his neck. He rode in the royal chariot, and before him the Egyptians ran shouting, as they do in the streets of Cairo to-day when any great person is driving through the crowded masses of men and beasts.

It was thirteen years since he had left his home, a shepherd boy in Canaan. Now he travelled all over the country, seeing that the grain was stored up in every large city of Egypt. And so the seven years of plenty passed by and the granaries of Egypt were full to overflowing.

The story of the Nile overflow, by which years of plenty and famine were decided, is a world-famed story, dating from the very dawn of history to the present day.

Let it be told yet once again.

CHAPTER 5

THE STORY OF THE NILE FLOOD

"The higher Nilus swells
The more it promises: as it ebbs, the seedsman
Upon the slime and ooze scatters his grain
And shortly comes to harvest."
—SHAKSPERE.

LET it be told once again—the story of how this great river, sometimes so shallow and sluggish that a child might safely walk across, becomes a mighty rushing sea pouring itself into the ocean, with a force that no man can stem.

The source of the Nile was as great a mystery to the men of old as was the reason of its yearly flood. So, as they could not find out where this great river rose, they said it must rise in Paradise, that it must flow through burning regions, pass through a sea, and finally make its way through Egypt.

The annual flood they explained to themselves by saying that it was caused by Isis, the Egyptian goddess, mourning for her brother Osiris. Every year, toward the middle of June, she let fall a

18

tear for the great Nile-god, and at once the river swelled and descended upon earth. This quaint old story has lasted down through all the ages, and to this very day the people in Egypt say that a drop from heaven falls during the night of the 18th of June and brings about the rise of the Nile. That night is known as the "night of the drop."

During the months of April, May, and June the river Nile falls and falls. The fields on either side are parched and dry; the air is full of dust. The trees are leafless, the plains are cracked; man and beast alike languish. And all day long the fiery sun, undimmed by the lightest cloud, marches on its pitiless way through a sky of the deepest blue. As the season advances, anxiety becomes intense.

"Will the river rise well this year?" ask the bronze-faced men one of another. "Is it not late already?"

A year of plenty or a year of famine used to hang on this mysterious rise. At last, the day dawns when news comes flashing along the river-banks: "The Nile is rising a little, away up near its source." Slowly—very slowly at first, and then with ever-increasing speed—the water creeps up its banks. Gradually the current quickens and the water becomes a deepened colour. It has now become a rushing mighty stream against which no man could swim, as it swirls and roars along to the sea.

And yet not a drop of rain has fallen, no cloud has crossed the sky, no storm has broken over the land. It is to tropical rains some two thousand miles away that this tumult of waters is due. By September the country is a huge lake, the whole land is a land of rivers, as it once was a land of dust. Men's spirits rise with the rising waters, the animals rejoice in this first necessity of life, brown-skinned men and boys plunge with delight into the life-giving stream. All are happy and content. For it will be a year of plenty for Egypt.

As September wears on, the river begins to fall. Its work is done. Before long it is flowing between its banks as usual, winding through the long hot land to the Great Sea—the "Very Green," as the men of Egypt called it.

We know a great deal about the sources of the Nile now, though it was many centuries before the discoveries were made. At Khartum—known to history for Gordon's famous defence and death—the great river divides into two branches, one called the Blue Nile, the other known as the White Nile.

It was in 1770 that a Scotch explorer named James Bruce reached the source-lakes of the Blue Nile, high up on the plains which crowned the mountains of Abyssinia. He told such wonderful stories on his return home of all he had seen and heard that people did not believe him. But now we know all he said was perfectly true. It was not till 1858 that two Englishmen discovered the source of the White Nile in Lake Victoria.

But it happened years ago that the tropical rains sometimes failed; the rise of the Nile was very poor, the dry earth remained parched and cracked, and famine was the result. So it was a very important matter to the old kings of Egypt whether the Nile rose well or not.

To-day famine is impossible, owing to the dykes, canals, and dams which have been arranged to hold the water should the Nile fail to rise well.

CHAPTER 6

IN A STRANGE LAND

"My sons, and ye the children of my sons,
Jacob your father goes upon his way."
—CLOUGH.

FOR the first seven years after Joseph had been made governor of Egypt, the Nile rose well, and every fifth part of the country's produce was stored up in the granaries of Egypt, and "in all the land of Egypt there was bread." The bad years came. The Nile did not rise, the corn did not grow, and the famished people cried to Pharaoh for bread.

"Go unto Joseph; what he saith to you, do," was Pharaoh's answer to all the clamouring people. And Joseph opened the storehouses of grain and sold to the Egyptians.

Not only was there famine in Egypt, but the famine was "over all the face of the earth." This included the land of Canaan, where Joseph's father and brothers still lived. There came a day, as the famine grew worse and worse, when Jacob called his sons.

"Behold, I have heard that there is corn in Egypt," he said to them: "get you down thither, and buy for us from thence; that we may live, and not die."

The ten brothers started off for Egypt to buy corn. They found that the governor was selling the corn in person. He was the great man of the land, and they bowed down themselves before him with their faces to the earth. They little thought that this man to whom every one bowed down was their young brother Joseph, but Joseph recognised his brothers at once. The sight of their familiar faces moved him strangely, and he turned from them in tears. He behaved generously towards them, but he did not tell them who he was. And when they had filled their sacks with corn they went home.

But the famine went on, and again they came, bringing Benjamin, the youngest son, with them this time. They brought Joseph presents too—honey and spices, nuts and almonds. Again they bowed low before him.

"Is your father well, the old man of whom ye spake? Is he yet alive?" were Joseph's eager words when he saw them again. Yet again he turned from them in tears, which they could not understand.

At last he told them who he was—told them simply, weeping and alone, "I am Joseph your brother, whom ye sold into Egypt."

Then he informed them that he was lord of Pharaoh's house, and a ruler throughout all the land of Egypt.

23

"And ye shall tell my father of all my glory in Egypt, and of all that ye have seen; and ye shall haste and bring down my father hither."

So the brothers journeyed back into Canaan, laden with good things from Egypt, to tell their father the good news.

"It is enough," said the old man; "Joseph my son is yet alive: I will go and see him before I die."

And Jacob left his old home, and he took his sons and his grandsons, and all their wives and children, his cattle and all his goods. It must have been a long line of camels and asses, together with the waggons that Pharaoh had sent from Egypt, that crossed the burning desert, to go down into Egypt. And Joseph drove out in his chariot to meet his father, and he fell on his neck and wept a good while."

Joseph brought his father into the presence of the great Pharaoh, and the king treated the old man well, giving him a portion of land to dwell in Goshen between Memphis and the Great Sea, at the delta of the Nile. It was one of the best pieces of land in Egypt, and there Jacob settled down with his sons and his grandsons, their wives and children, to live in peace and plenty.

Now Jacob was already old when he came down into the land of Egypt. And when the time came for him to die, his one yearning was to get back to his old home. He could not rest in the land of the pyramids. The Egyptians were kind, but they

"Thou shalt carry me out of Egypt."

were not his own kin; he felt he must lie in the land of his fathers.

"Bury me not, I pray thee, in Egypt," he pleaded with Joseph: "but I will lie with my fathers, and thou shalt carry me out of Egypt, and bury me in their burying-place."

So Jacob died, and the Egyptians mourned for him, as if he had been one of themselves; after which his whole family carried him home to the land of his birth. It was a very great company that bore him to Canaan; the camels and asses of the house of Jacob, mingling strangely with the chariots and horses of the Egyptians.

So they buried him in the land of Canaan, as he had desired them, and then Joseph and all his brethren returned to their new home in Egypt.

CHAPTER 7

THE CHILDREN OF ISRAEL

"Unto a land flowing with milk and honey."
—EXODUS iii. 8.

THE children of Jacob, or Israel, lived long in the land of Egypt, on the plot of land given to them by Pharaoh. Fifty-four years after his father, Joseph died. Like Jacob, he yearned to be buried in the land of his fathers, but for the present this was impossible. The years rolled on, and king after king reigned and died in Egypt, until the memory of Joseph was forgotten.

Meanwhile the children of Israel were rejoicing in the good pasture-land watered by the Nile, the land of Goshen as it was called, between Memphis and the Great Sea, and their families increased, till they had become quite a large colony in the land of Egypt. But in course of time there arose a Pharaoh, who no longer cared to have all Joseph's descendants settled in the land; this great colony of foreigners would be a danger in case of war.

So he set taskmasters over them and oppressed them. He took them away from their quiet shepherd lives, to "service in the field," such as we still see along the banks of the Nile. There to-day the peasants work under the burning sun, drawing up buckets of water, from the level of the river, to pour on the fields above. The children of Israel were made to build the high brick walls, too, which surrounded the old cities of the land of Goshen; they were treated as slaves, and beaten by the Egyptians in authority over them, until we seem to hear their bitter cries, for deliverance from this bondage.

At last, as more and more children were born to the children of Israel, Pharaoh ordered that all the sons born to these strangers should henceforth be thrown into the Nile.

But a son was born, soon after this order, to a great grandson of Jacob's, and he was so beautiful, that his mother hid him in the house, for three months. Then, fearing for his life, she put him in a little boat or basket made of reeds, and laid him away among the rushes, by the river-side.

The story of Moses is well known, and every child has heard how the royal princess, one of Pharaoh's daughters, came down with her maidens, to bathe in the river. How she found the little basket and the crying child within, and how she had not the heart to let the baby drown. How he was nursed by his own mother, brought up in the house of the Egyptian princess, and named Moses: "Because," said the princess, "I drew him out of the water."

Now, though Moses was brought up as an Egyptian child, he was yet an Israelite at heart; when he grew old enough he resented seeing his own people badly treated, and even beaten, in the land of their adoption. And this was the man chosen to lead his own people from the land of Egypt, back to their own land—the land given to their forefathers Abraham and Jacob—the land of Canaan.

The story of their start for home is very picturesque. One can see the shepherd tribes of Goshen snatching their last hasty meal; their feet, usually bare, now shod for their long journey; men, women, and children with staffs in their hands, their long Eastern garments girt up round their waists, for walking over the sandy desert.

It was night too; probably one of those glorious African nights, with stars shining out brightly, even as they shine to-day over stretches of veldt, while the moon lit up the country round.

"Get you forth from among my people; also take your flocks and herds, as ye have said, and be gone," were the words wrung at last from the reluctant Pharaoh, who had so long refused to let them go.

So in that quiet starlit night, the children of Israel, like a huge army, with their camels and asses, stole forth from Egypt, on their way back to their fatherland.

Very soon the green pasture-land of the Nile was left behind; the scorching desert track lay before.

Encamped by the shores of the Red Sea, suddenly a cry of alarm would run through the vast multitude, as across the ridges of the desert hills came the terrible Egyptian chariots pursuing after them. In the midst of their terror the sun sank down, and darkness fell over the waters of the Red Sea, which cut them off from the land of Canaan. The story of their crossing over is too well known to repeat. When morning broke over the hills of Arabia, they stood in safety on the farther shore, but the chariots and horsemen of Egypt had perished in the waters.

CHAPTER 8

BACK TO THE FATHERLAND

"Shout, Israel. Let the joyful cry
Pour forth the notes of victory,
High let it swell across the sea,
For Jacob's weary tribes are free."
—RUSKIN (aged thirteen)

FOR two hundred and fifteen years the Israelites had lived in Egypt. Now they had passed from Africa, into Asia. Not one of them could remember Jacob now, or his long journey down into Egypt. Behind— right across the waters—lay the strange land of their exile, the land of Egypt with its life-giving river, its pyramids, its stone statues, its tyrant kings. Behind, lay the endless stir and life of the busy Egyptians, with their trained armies marching through their walled cities, their vast processions with drums and cymbals, the rumble of their horses and chariots.

Before them lay mile after mile of burning desert land, through the deep silence of which, they must march, day after day, week after week, month after month. Now and then they might rest by some spring of water to refresh themselves and their little ones, their camels and their asses. But onward and ever onward they pressed towards the land of Canaan.

For months they wandered thus, now deeper and deeper into the mountains, struggling over rugged passes, till they reached the desolate range of the hills of Sinai. From these heights their leader Moses brought to them the code of laws, by which they were to live, the code of laws by which we live to-day—the Ten Commandments.

After a long stay in the desert land of Sinai, the six hundred thousand exiles set forth once more on their weary march north, to Canaan. It must have been a great day, when they first caught sight of the river Jordan, across which lay their new country, even though across that river their leader Moses was not to lead them.

The story of his death is perhaps one of the saddest in history. Encamping his people in the plain below, he went up into a high mountain from which he could see the land he was never to reach. Beneath him lay the black tents of the Israelites, behind him the weary waste of hot sand and the bitter waters; while away across the river Jordan he could see the land of Canaan stretching away to the sea—the good land "flowing with milk and honey," the land for which he had gladly borne toils and dangers, for which he, too, had hungered and thirsted.

It was his last view. From that mountain-top he came down no more. In that strange land he died, and another man was chosen to lead on the people.

"Moses went up into a high mountain, from which he could see the land
he was never to reach."

Joshua was a simple, straightforward, undaunted soldier—"strong and of a good courage." He turned neither to the right hand nor to the left hand. At the head of the hosts of Israel he went right forward from Jordan to Jericho, from Jericho to Ai, onwards and onwards, till his work was done, and the children of Israel had conquered the Promised Land.

It stretched from the river Euphrates, from the banks of which Abraham had wandered so long ago, right away to the river of Egypt,—the Nile, while its shores were washed by the Great Sea, the value of which, as yet, they knew not.

It was the highway between the two great rivals of the Old World; the only road by which they could approach each other, by which alone, the Chaldeans could get to Egypt, and the Egyptians to Chaldea, lay along the broad flat strip of coast belonging to Canaan.

What a land this was to possess! After the weary march of forty years, through the lonely desert, after the daily struggle for existence, after the hunger, the thirst, the anxiety, and long, delayed hope, the new fatherland must have been very welcome. Very welcome the shade of palm-tree and olives, of vineyards and fruit-trees, welcome the hills and ravines, the gushing spring and green plains. There were cattle, sheep, and goats on the hillsides; there were waving cornfields in the sunny plains; there were flowers blooming in the early summer when they first arrived, and bees swarming round their combs in rock and wood.

No wonder, then, the way-worn travellers should love to dwell on the words that had cheered them through the weariness of the way; to them it was indeed "a land flowing with milk and honey, the glory of all lands."

CHAPTER 9

THE FIRST MERCHANT FLEET

"They that go down to the sea in ships,
that do business in great waters."
—PSALM cvii. 23.

NOW, it has been said that the waters of the Great Sea, washed the shores of the land of Canaan, into which, the Israelites had just entered. Let us see what this Great Sea is, and how the people who lived on the coast of Canaan, found out, how to sail on its calm surface. Seeing branches of trees and leaves floating down the river, they first got the idea of floating down themselves on a log.

Then followed the notion of guiding themselves by means of a pole or paddle. Sometimes the log was hollowed out, sometimes covered by an inflated skin. By-and-by a number of logs, placed together, suggested the idea of a raft, for carrying a number of persons or animals across a river. These were the rude beginnings of shipbuilding, in the olden days. They soon added the idea of oars for propelling the rafts, using them in the same way, that a duck uses its legs to swim.

Then they found that sometimes the wind helped them, so they made sails—that is to say, they spread sheets of linen to catch the wind, and blow the ship forwards. They were ever thinking of something fresh, until at last they gathered up enough courage to trust themselves on the sea itself.

The Egyptians first tried the Red Sea, which washes the east coast of Africa. It was a narrow arm of the sea, more like a very broad river, save that it was salt, and there were no large waves.

While the Israelites were yet groaning under their bondage in the land of Egypt, there reigned a queen called Hatasu, or "Queen of the South and North," as she was more often called. She caused a great fleet to be built on the shores of the Red Sea. Each ship was built with oars and sails, each capable of holding sixty passengers. Of these, thirty were the rowers, who were to plough the waves and bring the ships to land whether the wind were favourable or not.

The object of the expedition was to trade with another part of East Africa, that could not well be reached by land. There were men-at-arms in each ship, in case hostile tribes hindered them in their trade dealings.

Away started the ships,—five of them,—and favourable winds bore them southwards to the land of Punt, or Somaliland, as we call that tract of country to-day. The voyagers were well received by natives, who were trustful people. The Egyptians soon found the chief of the country. He had a dwarf wife, who was very distressing to behold; but the royal couple proved very friendly; they were charmed with the presents from Egypt, and allowed the new-comers to trade freely.

They had leave to enter the forests, cut down the trees, and carry them to the ships. They dug up thirty-one of these trees, and placed them on the ships' decks, screening them from the sun's rays by an awning. Other things were brought to the beach by the natives, who were ready to exchange gold, silver, ivory, ebony, and other woods for the gifts brought to them from Egypt. Monkeys, dogs, leopard-skins, and slaves, were also put on board, and the Queen of Punt herself insisted on accompanying the ships back to Egypt.

The Egyptians seem to have been much amused by the antics of the monkeys on the voyage home, as they sprang about the sails and rigging of the ships. While the ships returned to the harbour in the Red Sea from which they had sailed, some of the cargo, including the trees, were taken across the desert, shipped on Nile boats, and so carried to Thebes. The day of the return of the expedition was kept as a gala day in the city of Thebes. A large number of the townspeople came out to meet the returning travellers, and the poor little Queen of Punt, did homage to the Queen of Egypt.

The complete success which had attended this first sea-adventure pleased Hatasu immensely, and she celebrated the event by building a new temple at

Thebes, on the walls of which were painted the chief scenes of the expedition.

Here may be seen, even to-day, the most ancient pictures of sea-going ships that the world contains—pictures of the Queen of Punt and the chiefs, the crews of the ships, the arrival of the expedition at Thebes in twelve large Nile boats, and the grand festival held in honour of the safe return of the fleet.

CHAPTER 10

CONQUERORS OF THE SEA

"My purpose holds
To sail beyond the sunset and the baths
Of all the western seas until I die."
—TENNYSON, Ulysses.

NOW when the six hundred thousand children of Israel came trooping into the land of Canaan, there were a great many tribes already living there. Amongst others there was a large tribe, known as the Phœnicians, living in the extreme north. They occupied a narrow strip of coast land between the high snow-capped mountains of Lebanon and the Great Sea.

It was simpler for them to trade by sea than to reach the inland country over the mountains of Lebanon—a journey which had to be accomplished on mules. The smiling sea which lay in front of them, invited them to trust themselves to its calm surface. The island of Cyprus was plainly visible across the waters, offering them safe harbours in case of sudden storms.

So the Phœnicians learnt the value of the sea, and by reason of this, they rose to fame and played a large part in the history of the world. It must have required some courage to sail even on the tideless waters of the Great Sea, in those early days, for, as we have already seen, the ships were very untrustworthy. They were not like the magnificent steamships, that put to sea in all weathers from every navigable port in these days.

Here is the story of a shipwreck, that took place before Joseph was sold into Egypt, and which shows how terrified the Eastern people were of venturing on the sea.

"I set sail," says the shipwrecked sailor, "in a vessel one hundred and fifty cubits long and forty wide, with one hundred and fifty of the best sailors of Egypt, whose hearts were more resolute than lions. They had foretold, that the wind would not be contrary, or that there would be none at all; but a squall came on unexpectedly, while we were in the open, and as we approached land the wind freshened and raised waves to the height of eight cubits. As for me, I clung to a beam, but those who were on the vessel perished, without one escaping. A wave cast me on an island, after having spent three days alone with no other companion than my own heart. I slept there in the shade of a thicket, then I set my legs in motion in quest of something for my mouth."

Now, when the new Israelite tribes began to sweep over the country, the tribes already in the land were pushed towards the coast, and the little strip known as Phœnicia became very much overcrowded. This gave a new life to their enterprise.

Up to this time they had sailed from headland to headland along their coast, under the friendly shelter of their tall mountains—sailed in their home-made boats, handling with skill their "sea-horses," as they called them, when they rode from shore to shore.

Their one idea had been to trade—to exchange the products of their own country for the products of those beyond the seas.

Now their own country was too full, they must go in search of settlement where some of their people could go and live; they must find ports and harbours, points good for trade, where their kinsmen might barter and sell the products of the old country.

The island of Cyprus had long ago attracted the Phœnicians. They could see its clear outline on fine summer evenings in the glow of the western sky; they could sail with ease and safety, keeping land in sight all the way. Thither it was natural that their eyes should turn when in search of a colony.

Beyond Cyprus, too, to the smaller island of Rhodes they ventured, and steering through unknown seas, they discovered Sicily.

Farther and yet farther they ventured.

Cutting down cedars, for which the mountains of Lebanon were famous, they built more and more ships, they added a greater number of oars, they made better sails.

Westward, and ever westward, they fought their way—battling with the wind and waves of the Great Sea—right along the coast of North Africa.

They would pass not a single town, they would meet not a single ship, unless it was one of their own. They did not know the currents of the sea, they had no means of knowing the force of the wind, they had no compass to guide them. The sun overhead was their only guide, the stars and the moon by night their only light.

They were indeed a brave people, and their success was richly deserved.

CHAPTER 11

EARLY PIONEERS

"Conquering, holding, daring, venturing, as we go the unknown ways,
Pioneers, O Pioneers!"

—W. WHITMAN.

ALONG the northern coast of Africa they kept, till they reached the spot known to the people of old as the "Pillars of Hercules." These were lofty rocks which were supposed to mark the limit of the world in this direction. It was, according to their ideas, the farthest point reached by the god Hercules. Beyond this point was the home of the gods, so they said, and heaven and earth met together. If they could please the gods, then the Phœnician sailors might pass this point and discover the truth of their belief; but either the sea was too rough for them or the sailors were too timid, for twice they returned home without having passed the Pillars.

Again they tried, and again they failed. At last a third fleet of Phœnician ships was fitted out; and this time they managed to pass through the narrow straits, and to penetrate the mysteries beyond.

There were no gods. The Pillars of Hercules were not the ends of the world. The rocky gates opened a path from the Great Sea, to the boundless waters of the Atlantic Ocean, which were to play such a great part in the history of the New World.

It was on this well-known voyage, that they founded the city of Gades, a port on the coast of Spain. Here they built a beautiful temple to the god Hercules, who had allowed them to pass the narrow straits. This city is our modern Cadiz, the most ancient town in all Europe.

The surrounding country they called Tarshish. Here they found a quantity of silver.

"The ships of Tarshish," says the prophet Ezekiel, to Phœnicia, "were thy caravans; so wert thou replenished, and very glorious in the midst of the sea."

So much silver, indeed, did the Phœnicians get at Tarshish, that, in order to carry home as much as they could, they made anchors of silver for their ships, leaving the old iron anchors behind.

"Rivers of the liquid metal, mountains of solid ore, forests and meadows covered with silver: silver,

silver, silver everywhere, in the land beyond the Pillars of Hercules," sang the old poets.

There is an old story that says, when the Phœnicians had passed through the Straits of Gibraltar, they took their course along the coast of Africa; but they were carried away far into the ocean by a strong wind. After being driven about many days by the storm, they came to a large island, which was so fertile and possessed such a glorious climate, that they thought it must be a dwelling for the gods, rather than of men.

They called them the "Isles of the Blessed." To-day we know these islands as the Canary and the Madeira Islands, and they are coaling-stations, for the great steamships which ply between England and South Africa, every week, in all weathers, throughout the year.

There is little doubt, that the old Phœnician ships got as far as the English Channel, in their search for wealth, braving the high seas of the Bay of Biscay to do this. Coasting along the shores of Spain and France, they reached the Scilly Isles off the coast of Cornwall—the Tin Islands, as they called them— in order to carry tin back to Phœnicia.

Thus Phœnicia became the mistress of the Great Sea.

Backwards and forwards, went the Phœnicians, between their own country and foreign lands, collecting wealth, planting colonies, taking possession of whole islands, undisputed. They improved their ships, they grew more and more adventurous, until their country, that narrow strip of land shut in between the mountains of Lebanon and the Great Sea, became very rich.

They were conquerors of the sea indeed, merchants of the people of many isles, strong to do and dare, the first Naval Power in the Old World.

CHAPTER 12

HIRAM, KING OF TYRE

"For Hiram was ever a lover of David."
—1 KINGS v.1.

So the Phœnicians were already a great seafaring people when the Israelites finally conquered Canaan and were united under their first king, Saul, though they had not reached the full height of their fame till Solomon became King of Israel.

Now, a great friendship had existed between David, the poet king of Israel, Solomon's father, and Hiram, the young king of Phœnicia. And when Hiram heard, that King David was going to build himself a palace, in his new capital of Jerusalem, Hiram sent him a present of newly felled cedar-trees from Lebanon, together with an offer of carpenters and masons, to help in the building. David accepted both, and the skilled workmen from Phœnicia came with their tools to Jerusalem and worked there. Hiram was ever a lover of David, but he was a yet greater friend of Solomon. A treaty of trade was soon established, between the two kingdoms of Israel and Phœnicia.

Here is the well-known story.

"And Hiram king of Tyre sent his servants unto Solomon; for he had heard that they had anointed him king in the room of his father: for Hiram was ever a lover of David. And Solomon sent to Hiram, saying, . . . Command thou that they hew me cedar-trees out of Lebanon; and my servants shall be with thy servants: and unto thee will I give hire for thy servants according to all that thou shalt appoint: for thou knowest that there is not among us any that can skill to hew timber like unto the Sidonians. . . . And Hiram sent to Solomon, saying, I have considered the things which thou sentest to me for: and I will do all thy desire concerning timber of cedar, and concerning timber of fir. My servants shall bring them down from Lebanon unto the sea; and I will convey them by sea in floats unto the place that thou shalt appoint me, and will cause them to be discharged there, and thou shalt receive them: and thou shalt accomplish my desire, in giving food for my household."

So Phœnicia supplied Israel with wood and craftsmen, and Israel supplied Phœnicia with corn and oil, year by year.

Phœnicia was growing richer and richer, and Hiram set to work to enlarge, adorn, and fortify his capital, Tyre, until it became one of the most beautiful and renowned cities, in the ancient world.

Tyre and Sidon were already of world-wide fame, when Hiram came to the throne of Phœnicia; but much was needed in the way of harbours for the ever-increasing shipping, and to this task he set himself.

Old Tyre lay on the sea-shore, but with the rapid growth of trade, the sailors of the old town, began to use the island which lay close by, and afforded excellent shelter to their ships. King Hiram had this island enlarged and surrounded by strong walls, which ran out sharply into the sea. Then he built two harbours,—one to the north, looking towards Sidon; the other to the south, looking towards Egypt,—so that in bad weather, when the waves rose high and the winds blew, the merchants of Tyre could reach a safe port.

Above the city itself rose battlements and towers. Pleasant houses lay amid gardens and orchards, shaded by vines and olives. With ivory and ebony, with gold and silver, with precious stones and jewels, Tyre was beautified.

"The king of Tyre sits like a god in the seat of God," sings Ezekiel, "in the midst of the seas. He dwells as in Eden. Precious stones are the covering of his palaces."

The wonderful mixture of land and sea is picturesquely described by an old poet: "The sailor furrows the sea with his oar, as the ploughman the soil: the lowing of oxen and the song of birds, answer the deep roar of the main: the breeze from Lebanon, while it cools the rustic at his midday labour, speeds the sailor seaward."

CHAPTER 13

KING SOLOMON'S FLEET

"And King Solomon made a navy of ships . . .
on the shore of the Red Sea."
—1 KINGS ix. 26.

NOW when Solomon had finished building the wonderful temple at Jerusalem, he turned his attention to other parts of his dominions. He had learned much from the Phœnicians; he saw the wealth that poured yearly into Tyre, and he felt that a navy for his own people, would greatly tend to improve foreign trade and commerce.

True he had, by his marriage with the daughter of Pharaoh, King of Egypt, improved the trade-routes between the two countries of Egypt and Canaan. But the power of the sea was beginning to make itself felt through the Eastern world, and Solomon appealed to Hiram for help.

Now, the Phœnicians had no port on the shores of the Red Sea, and very gladly Hiram seems to have thrown himself into the scheme for building a new navy for Solomon. To the chosen port, King Solomon travelled himself, to arrange about the making of the fleet. "The Giant's Backbone," as the port was called, was soon teeming with life and activity, shipbuilders from Tyre, and sailors from the land of Phœnicia, were hard at work preparing the new ships, until at last the great fleet was ready to sail forth.

Guided by Phœnician pilots, manned by Phœnician sailors, Phœnicians and Israelites sailed forth together on their mysterious voyages, into the southern seas. They sailed to India, to Arabia and Somaliland, and they returned with their ships laden with gold and silver, with ivory and precious stones, with apes and peacocks.

The amount of gold brought to Solomon by his navy was enormous. Silver was so abundant, as to be thought nothing of in those days, and all the king's drinking-cups and vessels were of wrought gold, and every three years his fleet returned with yet more and more gold and silver.

For the first time, too, we can see the beginning of contact between the West and East.

"The kings of Tarshish and of the isles shall bring presents," sang the Psalmist. This was from the West, from the Tarshish in Spain, already discovered by the Phœnician sailors, the Tarshish from whence pure silver flowed in glowing streams.

"The kings of Sheba and Seba shall offer gifts," sang the Psalmist again. This was from the East, from the shores of Arabia, from the yet more distant coasts of India, now opened up for the first time in history. "Yea, all kings shall fall down before

51

him; all nations shall serve him." So it was the Phœnicians that taught the Israelites, how to attain all this splendour and riches, insomuch as they taught them the value of the sea.

Now, though the Phœnicians were the first pioneers of the sea, yet they did not neglect their homework. They excelled in bronze work and ivory carving. There are two bronze gates now to be seen in England, carved by these old Phœnicians; they are covered with groups of figures busy with all the occupations of a seaport.

Tyrian dyes, too, were renowned throughout the ancient world. Here is the old story of how they discovered the purple dye.

It was in the old, old days,—so they said,— that one day the nymph Tyros was walking by the sea-shore with Hercules, her beloved. Suddenly her dog broke a small shell with his teeth, and his mouth immediately became dyed with a brilliant red colour. Tyros declared that unless Hercules would procure for her a robe of the same tint, he should see her face no more. Hercules gathered a number of the shells, and having dipped a garment in the blood of the shellfish, he presented it to Tyros, who was henceforth adorned with the royal purple, which throughout all ages has remained the royal colour for British kings and princes.

In mining, too, the Phœnicians were experts. They dug mines in Lebanon—their own mountains—then in the country now known as Rhodesia in South Africa.

While Phœnicia was still at the height of her fame, Hiram, King of Tyre, died. And still to-day, in far-away Syria, a grey weather-beaten tomb of unknown age, raised aloft on three rocky pillars, looks down from the hills above Tyre—looks over the city and over the sea beyond. It is pointed out by the natives, to those who visit the once famous land of Phœnicia, as the "tomb of Hiram."

CHAPTER 14

THE STORY OF CARTHAGE

"Attempt not to acquire that which may not be retained."

ONE of the largest of the Phœnician settlements was called Carthage, which was on the northern coast of Africa. There is an old legend about the founding of this ancient city which is very quaint.

One of the kings of Tyre died, leaving a son called Pygmalion and a daughter Dido, who was very beautiful. Though Pygmalion was but a boy when his father died, the Phœnicians made him king. His sister Dido married a very rich man, of whose wealth Pygmalion was very jealous. After a time he slew his brother-in-law, hoping to get the wealth he owned. But Dido hid the treasure. She was very sad and troubled, for she loved her husband, and she made up her mind to escape from the country. Taking many nobles of the city with her, she put all her riches on board one of her brother's ships and set sail for Cyprus secretly.

Now, when Pygmalion found that his sister had fled, taking some of his citizens with her, he was very angry and would have pursued her, but he was hindered by the prophets, who said—

"It will go ill with thee, if thou hinder the founding of that which shall be the most fortunate city in the whole world."

Then Dido sailed from Cyprus to the coast of Africa, landing some fifteen miles from Utica, which had long been a Phœnician colony. She found the natives on the coast friendly, and bought a piece of land, "so much as could be covered with the hide of an ox, that she might refresh her companions, who were now greatly wearied with their voyage."

Thither came many natives bringing merchandise for sale, and very soon there grew up a large town. The people of Utica claimed kindred with the newcomers, for were they not all from the old country Phœnicia? And they built up their beautiful city, and called it Carthage. The site was well chosen. The promontory, on which it stood, afforded excellent harbours for shipping, and the Phœnician settlers, anchoring in this haven, were not slow to see its advantages.

Midway in the Great Sea, within easy reach of Spain and Sicily, this new African town was indeed to be "the most fortunate city in the whole world."

Phœnicia was at the height of her power, Greece was not yet great, Rome had not risen. The great empires of the East, Egypt and Babylon, were slowly dying; Carthage was yet to rule the Great Sea and overshadow the mother country.

The city grew more and more flourishing. The beauty and fame of Dido were noised abroad until it reached the ears of the King of the Moors. He sent for the men of Carthage.

"Go back to the queen and say that I demand her hand in marriage," said the king; "and if she be not willing, then I will make war upon her and her city."

But these men, fearing to give Dido the king's message, knowing the love she bore her husband, invented a crafty device.

"The King of the Moors," they said, "desireth to find some one who shall teach his people a more gentle manner of life; but who shall be found that will leave his own kinsfolk and go to a barbarous people that are as the beasts of the field?"

Dido reproved them.

"No man should refuse to endure hardness of life, if it be for his own country's sake: nay, he must give his very life to it, if need be," she answered, with a patriotism rare in those early days.

Then the men of Carthage answered—

"Thou art judged out of thine own mouth, O queen. What therefore thou counsellest to others, do thyself, if thou wouldst serve thy country."

Dido had fallen into her own trap. She was very unhappy.

"Give me the space of three months," she said, "that I may lament my former estate."

Then she went to the farthest part of the city—the city of her own founding, destined to such great things. She had built a great funeral-pile, and one day she herself mounted it to the top, having a drawn sword in her hand.

Looking down upon the Carthaginians, who were gathered round, she cried aloud with a resolution born of despair—

"Ye bid me go to my husband. See, then, I go."

Thereupon she drove the sword into her heart, and fell down dead. Such is the legend of the founding of Carthage.

CHAPTER 15

OUT OF THE SHADOWLAND

"Worlds on worlds are rolling ever
From creation to decay."
—SHELLEY.

MEANWHILE the Phœnicians were still masters of the Great Sea, though their colony of Carthage was destined to outshine them in course of time.

Under Neco, King of Egypt, it is said, they attempted to sail right round Africa. Neco, with a view to commerce, wished the coast of Africa to be explored as far as possible, so he applied to the Phœnicians, as the first sailors of their day, for help. Had they not braved the terrors of the Atlantic, outside the Pillars of Hercules? Had they not manned Solomon's navy with their finest navigators?

The Phœnicians, as usual, seemed ready to go, and Neco started them off, from a port in the Red Sea, with orders to sail southwards, keeping the coast of Africa on their right, and to return to Egypt if possible by way of the Great Sea. There is some doubt among the old historians as to whether they succeeded or not.

Coasting along the shores of the Red Sea, they would pass through the narrow Straits of Bab-el-Mandeb and enter the Indian Ocean. So much they had already done; but instead of going off to India, they would hug the coast of East Africa, past Somaliland, Zanzibar, and Zululand, till they reached South Africa. How the Phœnician boats, with their many sails and oars, rounded the Cape of Storms, which defied the Portuguese sailor two thousand years later, is not related; but, according to the old story, they coasted up the west side of Africa, entered the Great Sea by the Straits of Gibraltar, and reached Egypt. It took them three years to perform the voyage, and Neco the king must have given them up as lost long ago, for he knew they had no food to last them so long. But the Phœnicians had been equal to the occasion. Every autumn they had landed on the coast, ploughed up a tract of land, sowed it with grain, and awaited the ripening of the corn the following spring.

And so, if this story be true, Africa was circumnavigated six hundred years B.C.

It seems strange to think that such a nation of adventurers should so completely have died out. Before relating the story of the fall of Phœnicia from her high pedestal of fame and glory, let us just glance at some of the quaint old stories of the childhood of Greece, that nation that should play such a large part in the history of the world.

While Moses was leading the children of Israel from Egypt to Canaan, and the men of Tyre were conquering the seas, Greece was beginning to awake from her legendary shadowland and to take her part in the world's struggles.

These people dwelt on the opposite shores of the Great Sea. Their broken coast faced North Africa, a little to the west of where the river Nile empties itself into the sea. Of course it was much too far to see across to the other side, so they imagined all sorts of things.

First, these old Greeks thought that there were twelve gods and goddesses who lived at the top of a real mountain called Olympus. They had not yet learnt, as the children of Israel had, that there was but one God over all. Their chief god they called Zeus, and he had a brother, Neptune, who was the god of the ocean. The goddess of the moon was called by them, Diana, the god of the sun Apollo. In the far east lived Aurora, the dawn, who opened the gates of the flat world with her rosy fingers, and out came the golden car of the sun with its glorious white horses. Then there was Venus, the goddess of beauty; Mars, the god of victory; Hercules, the god of strength, and a great many more. It was this god Hercules, who came to the end of the Great Sea, and set up the two pillars on each side of the Straits of Gibraltar, which cost the Phœnicians so much trouble to pass.

They had an old story, and a very strange one, which told of the peopling of their country.

A fair lady, they said, named Europa, was playing in the meadows on the coast of Phœnicia, between the mountains of Lebanon and the Great Sea. One day a great white bull came to her; he let her wreath his horns with flowers, lay down, and invited her to mount his back. No sooner had she done so than he rose, trotted down with her to the sea, and swam out of sight. He took her first to the island of Crete or Candia, not far from the coast of Greece; and as settlers came over there from the East, they called the name of the country after Europa, and it is known to this day by the name of Europe.

But this, like the story of Dido and the founding of Carthage, is but a legend made up by the old Greeks when they were creeping out of their shadowland.

CHAPTER 16

THE STORY OF THE ARGONAUTS

"The life of the Greeks is mirrored in their legends."

THESE old Greek stories, which were handed down from father to son, are a curious mixture of truth and romance, and no one knows which is which. Let us take their story of the Argonauts, when fifty of their heroes under the guidance of Jason, went off in search of the Golden Fleece. Here is the account of how they built their ship—an account which they must have taken from the Phœnicians:—

"Then they felled their pines and shaped them with an axe, and Argus, the famed shipbuilder, taught them to build a galley, the first long ship that ever sailed the seas. They pierced her for fifty oars, an oar for each hero of the crew, and pitched her with coal-black pitch, and painted her bows with vermilion, and they named her Argo, after Argus, and worked at her all day long.

"And at last the ship was finished, and they tried to launch her down the beach; but she was too

"They named her Argo, and worked at her all day long."

heavy for them to move her, and her keel sank deep into the sand.

"Then all the heroes looked at each other blushing, but Jason spoke and said, 'Let us ask the magic bough, perhaps it can help us in our need.' Then a voice came from the bough and bade Orpheus play upon the harp, while the heroes waited round, holding the pine-trunks, to help her towards the sea.

"Orpheus took his harp and began his magic song:—

" 'How sweet it is to ride upon the surges, and to leap from wave to wave, while the wind sings in the cheerful cordage and the oars flash fast among the foam! How sweet it is to roam across the ocean, and see new towns and wondrous lands, and to come home laden with treasure and to win undying fame!'

"And the good ship Argo heard him, and longed to be away and out at sea, till she stirred in every timber and heaved from stem to stern, and leapt up from the sand upon the rollers, and plunged onward like a gallant horse, and the heroes fed her path with pine-trunks till she rushed into the whispering sea.

"Then they stored her well with food and water, and pulled the ladder up on board, and settled themselves each man to his oar, and kept time to Orpheus's harp; and away across the bay they rowed southward, while the people lined the cliffs, and the women wept while the men shouted at the starting of that gallant crew.

"Jason was chosen captain, and each hero vowed to stand by their captain, faithfully, in the adventure of the Golden Fleece. And they rowed away over the long swell of the sea, past Olympus, and past the wooded bays of Athos, through the narrow straits, which led into the Sea of Marmora. Up the Bosphorus they went, to that land of bitter blasts, that land of cold and misery, and there was a battle of the winds, and the heroes trembled in silence as they heard the shrieking of the blasts. For the forest pines were hurled earthward, north and south, and east and west, and the Bosphorus boiled white with foam, and the clouds were dashed against the cliffs. And these dark storms and whirlwinds, haunt the Bosphorus until this day.

"Then the Argonauts went out into the open sea, which we now call the Black Sea. No Greek had ever crossed it, and all feared that dreadful sea, and its rocks, and shoals, and fogs, and bitter freezing storms. So the heroes trembled, for all their courage, as they came into that wild Black Sea and saw it stretching out before them without a shore, as far as the eye could see.

"But after a time they looked eastward, and midway between the sea and the sky they saw white snow-peaks hanging, glittering sharp and bright above the clouds. And they knew that they were come to Caucasus, at the end of all the earth; Caucasus, the highest of all mountains, the father of the rivers of the East. It was near here, amid the dark stems of the mighty beeches, that they saw the Golden Fleece.

"It would take too long to tell how Jason at last tore the fleece from off the tree-trunk, and how, holding it on high, he cried, 'Go now, good Argo, swift and steady, if ever you would see Olympus more.'

"And she went as the heroes drove her, grim and silent all, with muffled oars, till the pinewood bent like willow in their hands and stout Argo groaned beneath their strokes.

"On and on beneath the dewy darkness, till they heard the merry music of the surge upon the bar as it tumbled in the moonlight alone. Into the surge they rushed, and Argo leapt the breakers like a horse, for she knew the time was come to show her mettle, and win honour for the heroes and herself.

"Into the surge they rushed, and Argo leapt the breakers like a horse, till the heroes stopped, all panting, each man upon his oar, as she slid into the still broad sea. And the heroes' hearts rose high, and they rowed on stoutly and steadfastly, away into the darkness of the West.

"After many adventures in unknown seas they returned home again; but they were weary and spent with years of voyage; they had no strength to haul their boat on to the beach, so they sat and wept till they could weep no more. For the houses were all altered, the faces they saw were strange, and their joy was swallowed up in sorrow, while they thought of their youth and toil and the gallant comrades they had lost.

" 'Who are you that you sit weeping here?' asked the people at last.

" 'We are the sons of your princes, who sailed out many a year ago, to fetch the Golden Fleece, and we have brought it and grief therewith. Give us news of our fathers and mothers, if any of them be left alive.'

"Then there was shouting and laughing and weeping, and all the kings came to the shore, and they led the heroes to their homes. And Jason found his old father; but the old man would not believe it was his son, who had returned.

" 'Do not mock me, young hero,' he cried. 'My son Jason is dead at sea, long ago.'

" 'But I am your son Jason,' cried the hero. 'And I have brought home the Golden Fleece. Give me now the kingdom.'

"So all the heroes went their several ways, and that was the end of the story of the Argonauts."

CHAPTER 17

THE SIEGE OF TROY

"Far on the ringing plains of windy Troy."
—TENNYSON.

HERE is another story of these old heroic days before the dawn of history in Greece. And yet there is some truth in it, as there is in all these old stories. The city of Troy stood in the north-west corner of the land we now know as Asia Minor. It was therefore quite close to Greece.

This siege of Troy is supposed to have taken place, about the time that the children of Israel were settling down, under their first king, Saul.

Long, long ago, then, so the story runs, there was a King of Troy, called Priam. He had nineteen children, of whom Paris was the second. When Paris was old enough, he built a ship, and sailed away to visit the Greek kings. He made great friends with the King of Sparta, but he repaid his kindness, by stealing away his wife, the beautiful Helen.

As soon as the King of Sparta found how his hospitality had been misused, he called upon all the

Greek heroes to help him to recover his wife and to revenge himself on Paris. Every one replied to the call, and for many years, the Greeks collected their forces together. At last they were ready, and the King of Sparta's brother, Agamemnon, took command of them all.

With over a thousand ships and a hundred thousand men, the Greeks landed on the Trojan coast. They hauled their ships on shore, fastened them with ropes to large stones, which served as anchors, and surrounded the fleet with fortifications to protect it against the enemy. They fought the Trojans, with swords and spears. The chiefs generally, went to battle in a chariot, which was an open car drawn by two horses and driven by some trusty friend, who held the horses, while the chief stood up, and sent spear after spear, among the enemy.

The Greeks soon showed themselves to be superior to the Trojans, who shut themselves up within the huge walls of their city, leaving an opening on one side only, from which they might receive corn, cattle, and other supplies.

Nine summers and nine winters went by, and still the siege of Troy went on. The Greek heroes lost many of their finest men, but neither side would give in. The great hero among the Greeks was Achilles, among the men of Troy, Hector, the eldest son of old Priam. Both these were killed at last, and not very long after Paris himself was slain.

Still the King of Sparta could not get Helen back. Priam used to make her come and sit beside him on the battlements, over the gateway at Troy, to tell him the names of all the Greek chiefs.

But the King of Sparta grew desperate at last, and a means was devised for getting into Troy. Together with a number of Greek heroes, he hid himself in a monstrous wooden horse which was found on the sea-shore. Some one told the Trojans, if they would drag this wooden horse into Troy, their luck would turn, and it would bring them good fortune. So the Trojans harnessed themselves to the horse, and began to drag it into Troy, little thinking it was full of the enemy. Night came on, and suddenly at a given signal, the wooden horse was opened, and out tumbled the King of Sparta and his men, while outside, the other Greeks had seen the signal and rushed in.

Troy was set on fire, the King of Sparta rescued his beautiful wife and carried her down to his ship. Old Priam tried to put on his armour and defend his wife and daughters, but he was killed in the court of his palace. And all the rest of the men of Troy were either killed, or made slaves.

Only one great man of Troy escaped. That was Æneas, who, seeing that all was lost, took his old father on his back, and leading his little son by the hand, while his wife followed, escaped from the burning city. He found a ship on the coast and sailed away in safety.

After long years and marvellous adventures, he arrived on the shores of Italy, landing near the spot, where Rome now stands. It is said, that on the side of one of the mountains, he built a city, known as the Long White city; and here for three hundred years the descendants of Troy reigned.

So ended the great siege of Troy. It was first sung of, by the great poet Homer, in his wonderful poem called the 'Iliad'; but the acts of the heroes, have inspired many and many a poet since that time, until it has become one of the best known scenes, of the world's great history.

CHAPTER 18

THE ADVENTURES OF ULYSSES

"Come, my friends,
    'Tis not too late to seek a newer world.
    Push off, and sitting well in order, smite
The sounding furrows."
                        —TENNYSON.

WHEN the great city of Troy was taken, all the chiefs who had fought against it, set sail for their homes, though few of them returned in safety. One, who wandered farthest and suffered most, was Ulysses. He had brought twelve ships to Troy, and in each ship were fifty men; but that was ten years ago, and half his men slept their last sleep on the plains of Troy. This is some of his story as the Greek poet Homer tells it:

"Now Zeus, gatherer of the clouds, aroused the North Wind against our ships with a terrible tempest, and covered land and sea alike with clouds, and down sped night from heaven. Thus the ships were driven headlong, and their sails were torn to shreds by the might of the wind. So we lowered the sails into the hold, in fear of death, but rowed the ships landward, apace. There for two nights and two days, we lay continually, consuming our hearts with weariness and sorrow. But when the fair-tressed dawn had, at last, brought the full light of the third day, we set up the masts and hoisted the white sails and sat us down, while the wind and the helmsman guided the ships.

"And now I should have come to mine own country all unhurt, but the waves and the stream of the sea and the North Wind swept me from my course as I was doubling Cape Malea and drave me wandering past Cythera. Thence for nine whole days, was I borne by ruinous winds, over the teeming deep; but on the tenth day, we set foot on the land of the lotus-eaters, who eat a flowery food. So we stepped ashore and drew water, and when we had tasted meat and drink, I chose out two of my fellows to go and make search, what manner of men they were, who here live upon the earth, by bread. Then straightway they went and mixed with the men of the lotus-eaters, and the lotus-eaters gave them of the lotus to taste.

"Now whosoever of them did eat the honey-sweet fruit of the lotus had no more wish to bring tidings nor to come back, but there he chose to abide with the lotus-eating men, ever feeding on the lotus and forgetful of his homeward way. Therefore I led them back to the ships, weeping and sore, against their will, and dragged them beneath the benches and bound them in the hollow barks. So they embarked and sat upon the benches, and sitting orderly, they smote the grey sea with their oars.

"Thence we sailed onward, stricken at heart. And we came to the land of the Cyclopes (Sicily). These lawless folk dwell in hollow caves on the crests of the hills. Now, there is a waste isle stretching without the harbour of the land of the Cyclopes, wherein are wild goats unnumbered, for no path of man scares them, nor do hunters resort thither. Moreover, the soil lies evermore unsown and untilled, desolate of men, and feeds the bleating goats. Yet it is in nowise a sorry land, but would bear all things in their season; for therein, are soft water meadows by the shores of the grey salt sea, and there the vines know no decay, and the land is level to plough. Also there is a fair haven, where is no need of moorings, but men may run the ship on the beach, and tarry until such time, as the sailors are minded to be gone and favourable breezes blow."

Leaving Sicily, Ulysses came to the Isle of the Winds, which floated about in the ocean, and still he wandered on and on in the unknown seas. Here is his account of how his ship was struck by lightning: "But now, when we left that isle, nor any other land appeared but sea and sky, even then a dark cloud stayed above the hollow ship, and beneath it, the deep darkened. And the ship ran on her way for no long while, for, of a sudden, came the shrilling West, with the rushing of a great tempest, and the blast of wind snapped the two forestays of the mast, and the mast fell backward, and all the gear dropped into the bottom of the ship. And behold the mast struck the head of the pilot and brake all the bones of his skull together, and, like a diver he dropped down from the deck, and his brave spirit left his bones. In that same hour Zeus thundered and cast his bolt upon the ship, and she reeled all over, being stricken by the bolt of Zeus, and was filled with sulphur, and lo, my company fell out of the vessel.

"Like seagulls, they were borne round the black ship upon the billows and never returned. I kept pacing through my ship till the surge loosened the sides from the keel, and the waves swept her along, stript of her tackle, and brake her mast clean off at the keel. Then I lashed together both keel and mast, and sitting thereon, I was borne by the ruinous winds."

All night he drifted, rowing with his hands, until he was cast on to an island where he had to remain for the next eight years. Homer, the blind old poet, gives a touching account of his home-coming at last. Ulysses returned as a beggar, broken down, weary, and footsore. None knew him again, neither his old father, nor his son Telemachus, nor his wife Penelope, only his poor old dog Argus knew him, and he just licked his tired feet and died of joy.

CHAPTER 19

THE DAWN OF HISTORY

"The isles of Greece, the isles of Greece."
—BYRON.

WHILE the heroic age of Greece is passing with its memories of the Argonauts, the siege of Troy, and the adventures of Ulysses, let us take a look at the country, which was destined to become so great a power in the world.

One glance at the map will show, that Greece was cut up into little States. Why was this? Greece is naturally cut up into little pieces by its mountains, and deeply indented by its sea. One part is entirely divided from another part, by deep ravines with steep sides, and across these ravines no man could walk. Intercourse, therefore, between such a people was very difficult, often impossible.

See how different Greece is from Egypt. Egypt is a rich flat land stretching away on either side of the river Nile. The Egyptians could sail up the Nile with the wind, and drop down it, with the current, so that it was always quite easy to go from one part to another.

And so it was that from the very earliest times Egypt was one country under one king, like the Pharaohs of Bible history.

In Greece it was all different. There is no one flat tract of land anywhere. The great ranges of mountains divide it into a number of small districts, and each of these districts must have its own chief or king. These old Greeks were a free and hardy race, full of imagination and adventure, loving their old stories, loving their mountains, their sea, their freedom. Further than this, they enjoyed a climate which would breathe life into the dullest race; a climate, that clothed their mountains and islands with a beauty, of which their poets have ever loved to sing, which has raised them to that keen sense of beauty and art famous, throughout all ages.

To such a people, shipping became a necessity. They would learn the art of shipbuilding from the Phœnicians, who had long since made a settlement on the rocky crag, rising from out the plain known as the Acropolis, or Rock City. Thither came the Phœnicians, when the Greeks were but mere farmers, until very soon, on the Greek coast too, a new and busy life began. The Greeks had much to learn from the seafaring men from Tyre and Sidon, who came more and more to the Greek coasts, exchanging their own goods for Grecian products. In time the Greeks on the coast came to know all the Phœnicians knew: they took their alphabet, their weights and measures; they made ships like those used by the Phœnicians, and began to sail along their own shores.

It was therefore somewhat natural, that after a time the Greeks should turn their eyes eastwards across the blue waters, now known as the Archipelago, to the fertile shores of Asia Minor. Vast fields of rich grain and orchards of fruit, tempted the new settlers, until shipload after shipload had left the mother country, and scattered themselves along the opposite shores of Asia Minor, known as Ionia.

There is an old story of this Ionian migration, which says, that a certain king in Greece died, and his sons, not caring to live on in a country, where they could not live as princes, decided to leave it. They assembled at the Acropolis while their ships were preparing, and after a tedious voyage across the Archipelago, they landed on the coast of Asia Minor. They soon began to build cities, and before long, there were no less than twelve beautiful seaport towns on the Ionian coast belonging to Greece.

The chief of these were Miletus and Ephesus, both of which we shall hear of again. Miletus was stoutly defended by the natives already living there, which so enraged the Greeks that they slew every man they found and made the widowed women their wives. Legend relates, that the women were so heart-broken at this conduct, that they refused to sit at meat with their new husbands, or to call them by their names.

Ephesus rose to great importance as a seaport, and was also famous for the wonderful temple built to the goddess Diana, a worship which filled St Paul with such sorrow, when he spent three years among these Ephesians.

These towns had their day; they rose and fell, and nothing remains of them to-day, save reedy swamps and fever-stricken haunts, where once arose a perfect forest of masts, belonging to the ships trading with all parts of the then known world.

CHAPTER 20

THE FALL OF TYRE

"Is this your joyous city, whose antiquity is of ancient days?"
—ISAIAH xxiii. 7.

So the Greek nation slowly arose on the shores of the Great Sea, and by-and-by the colonies founded by Phœnicia, in Greece, had to be given up one by one. No longer were the Phœnicians free to come and go, to buy and sell, along the opposite shores. Greek cities rose, Greek ships put to sea, Phœnician colonies became Greek colonies.

But if a dangerous rival had appeared by sea, a yet more dangerous one had appeared by land. Nebuchadnezzar was King of Babylon, and Babylon was growing very powerful and strong. And this great king came down from the north, with chariots and horses and much people; he captured Sidon, laid low Jerusalem, and then came to reduce the renowned old city of Tyre.

For the last time, through the piercing eyes of Ezekiel, we seem to see Tyre, the old queen of commerce, in all her ancient glory:—

80

"The ships of Tarshish were thy caravans for thy merchandise:
And thou wast replenished, and made very glorious
    in the heart of the sea.
Thy rowers have brought thee into great waters:
The east wind hath broken thee in the heart of the sea.
And all that handle the oar, the mariners,
    and all the pilots of the sea,
They shall come down from their ships,
    they shall stand upon the land;
And shall cause their voice to be heard over thee,
    and shall cry bitterly.

       .   .   .   .

And they shall weep for thee in bitterness of soul
    with bitter mourning.
And in their wailing they shall take up a lamentation for thee,
And lament over thee, saying, Who is there like Tyre,
Like her that is brought to silence in the midst of the seas?"

And Nebuchadnezzar made forts against Tyre; he set his battering engines against her walls—those walls that Hiram had built so strong. He broke down her towers; her walls shook at the noise of his horsemen, when he entered into her gates. With the hoofs of his horses he trod down all her streets; he slew her people with the sword; he took her gold and silver, broke down her walls, destroyed her pleasant houses, while her timber from Lebanon, he cast into the waters.

Well, indeed, might the prophet Isaiah cry, "Howl, ye ships of Tarshish; for your strong place is laid waste."

Phœnicia fell in the year 574 B.C.

So busy had they been with the vast expansion of their trade on the seas that they had neglected home defence; when invasion came, they were powerless. Again, they had collected great wealth, but they had no worthy use for it. They did not understand, that wealth, if used aright, is but a means to nobler ends. To the Phœnicians it was an end in itself. The old Egyptian civilisation had not affected them, the wondrous new beginnings of Greek art did not appeal to them. They were the conquerors of the sea, the first colonisers in the Old World, and as such will always be remembered.

They have been compared to a flower that has bloomed too much and withered at its root; but the work was done, the seed had fallen in many places.

They vanished from the pages of history, leaving but memories behind, and now the tideless waters of the Mediterranean Sea lap peacefully over the old cities of Tyre and Sidon, while the world-famed Phœnicia of ancient days plays no part in the busy world of commerce which has shifted westwards.

CHAPTER 21

THE RISE OF CARTHAGE

"Because ye are Sons of the Blood and call me Mother still."
—KIPLING.

WHILE the mother country, Phœnicia, was falling, by reason of Nebuchadnezzar's siege of Tyre, her young colony of Carthage, was rapidly springing into fame. She was destined to eclipse even the glories of Tyre. Once indeed,—not long after the fall of Tyre,—while Carthage was busy extending her dominions, she had a narrow escape from destruction.

Cambyses, King of Persia, had conquered Egypt with such ease, that he was looking about for another country to lay low. Carthage was great enough to prove a danger, so he determined to march against that city. But it was two thousand miles away by land, and by sea alone could he hope to reach it. His fleet was made up of Phœnician ships, and manned by Phœnician sailors. These refused to take part in the expedition against their own kith and kin.

"We are bound to the Carthaginians," they said, "by solemn oaths. They too are our children, and it would be wicked to make war against them." And Cambyses had to be content with this answer, and give up his cherished plan of reducing Carthage.

Like the Phœnicians, the Carthaginians soon established colonies across the seas; but they took care to protect them. The Great Sea was no longer free to them to come and go as they liked. Greek ships sailed the seas, Greek colonies had sprung up along the coasts.

Nevertheless they owned colonies on the coast of Africa; the islands of Sardinia, Malta, and Corsica were theirs, they owned the group of Balearic Islands, while a great part of Southern Spain was under their rule. They had inherited a spirit of commerce from the parent State.

So the colony of Carthage had all the energy and trading instincts of the mother country. She held her own on the Great Sea, at a time when rival ships were sailing the sea, and Greece and Rome were clamouring for ports and colonies around the coast. She held her own till greed of conquest seized her, and in trying to get more than she could keep, she fell.

The story of her fall will be told later.

CHAPTER 22

HANNO'S ADVENTURES

"Tides duly ebbed and flowed,
Stars rose and set,
And new horizons glowed."
—TENNYSON.

Now Carthage can boast of having produced the first real explorer who has written an account of his doings. His name was Hanno. This Hanno was given command of a fleet of ships, to go and found a chain of colonies on the Atlantic sea-board of Africa. He took sixty ships and some thirty thousand men and women, who were to settle along the coast. When he came back to Carthage he wrote an account of the voyage, which was inscribed on a marble tablet and placed in the temple of the city; and this is what he said:—

"It was decreed, by the Carthaginians, that Hanno should sail beyond the Pillars of Hercules and found cities. Accordingly he sailed, with sixty ships of fifty oars each, and a multitude of men and women to the number of thirty thousand, and provisions and other equipment.

"When we had set sail and passed the pillars, after two days' voyage, we founded the first city. Below this city lay a great plain. Sailing thence westward we came to Cape Cantin, a promontory of Africa thickly covered with trees. Here we built a temple, and proceeded thence half a day's journey eastward, till we reached a lake, lying not far from the sea, and filled with abundance of great reeds. Here elephants were feeding and a great number of other wild animals.

"After we had gone a day's sail beyond the lakes, we founded cities near to the sea. Sailing thence, we came to a great river which flows from Africa. On its banks wandering tribes were feeding their flocks. With these we made friendship, and remained among them certain days. Beyond these dwell the 'inhospitable Æthiopians,' inhabiting a country that abounds in wild beasts, and is divided by high mountains. After this, sailing up a great river (the Senegal), we came to a lake. Proceeding thence a day's sail, we came to the farthest shore of the lake. Here it is overhung by great mountains, in which dwell savage men, clothed with the skins of beasts. These drove us away, pelting us with stones, so that we could not land.

"Sailing thence, we came to another river great and broad, and full of crocodiles and river-horses. Thence returning, we came back again to Herne, and from Herne, we sailed again towards the south for twelve days, coasting along the land. The whole of this land is inhabited by Æthiopians.

"On the last day, we came near to certain large mountains, covered with trees, and the wood of these trees was sweet-scented and of divers colours. Sailing by these mountains, for the space of two days, we came to a great opening of the sea, and on either side of this sea, was a great plain, from which, at night, we saw fire arising in all directions. Here we watered, and afterwards sailed for five days until we came to a great bay, which the interpreters told us, was called the Western Horn.

"In this bay was a large island. Here we landed, and in the daytime we could find nothing, but saw wood-ashes; but in the night we saw many fires burning, and heard the sound of flutes, and cymbals, and drums, and the noise of confused shouts. Great fear then came upon us. We sailed, therefore, quickly thence, being much terrified, and passing on for four days, found at night a country full of fire. In the middle was a lofty fire, greater than all the rest, so that it seemed to touch the stars. When day came, we found that this was a great mountain which they call the Chariot of the gods. On the third of our departure thence, having sailed by streams of fire, we came to a bay which is called the Southern Horn (close to Sierra Leone).

"At the end of this bay lay an island with a lake, and full of savage people, of whom the greater part were women. Their bodies were covered with hair, and our interpreters called them Gorillas. We pursued them; but the men we were not able to catch, for being able to climb the precipices, and defending themselves with stones, these all escaped.

But we caught three women. But when these, biting and tearing those that led them, would not follow us, we slew them, and flaying off their skins, carried these to Carthage.

"Farther we did not sail, for our food failed us."

CHAPTER 23

SOME MORE ABOUT GREECE

"Two voices are there: one is of the sea,
One of the mountains; each a mighty voice.
In each from age to age thou didst rejoice;
They were thy chosen music, Liberty."
—WORDSWORTH.

WHILE Carthage is growing day by day, and year by year, to take her place among the peoples, round the Mediterranean Sea, let us return to Greece, now taking a far larger part in the world's history, than Carthage would ever take.

A little inland, on the western coast of Southern Greece, was a wide and beautiful plain. It was watered by a flowing stream and shaded by well-wooded mountains. The spot was called Olympia, and it was dedicated to the worship of the great god Zeus. To this place every fourth year flocked the men of Greece, in olden times, to take part in the great festival, held in the god's honour. Games were the chief feature of the festival.

There was an old story saying that Hercules, when a little boy, had here won a foot-race with his brothers, so some of the Greeks in the south, founded this feast, with foot-races, for all the people to take part in. There were chariot-races and horse-races as well as foot-races; boxing-matches, wrestling, throwing weights, singing and reciting of poetry, so that all might have a chance.

The only prize given to the winners was a garland of wild olive, cut from a sacred tree in the grove. The victors were thus crowned before the people, each holding a palm branch in his hand, while the heralds proclaimed his name and that of his father and country.

From north and south, and east and west, the men of Greece flocked to Olympia. It was a bond of union, for all the scattered tribes of Greece. It helped the colonies to keep in touch with the mother country. It made a centre where men of all parts could meet and discuss matters of importance, and it gave a feeling of brotherhood to those, who were separated by the natural barriers of their divided country.

Now, amongst the chief people who attended these games, every four years at Olympia, were the Spartans. They lived in the south of Greece, and they were supposed to be the descendants of Hercules, and to have settled there, after their return from the siege of Troy. These Spartans were a very strict people, every citizen was a soldier. If a child were born weak or unhealthy, legend said, it was laid out on the wild slopes of the mountain-side to die. Only the strong and healthy were allowed to live.

So the Spartans became a very strong people. When seven years old, a boy was taken from his home, he was taught to endure hardships, and trained to love his country. At twenty he became a soldier and lived under stern discipline. The one aim of his life, was to become a good soldier; he existed for the State alone. His food was of the plainest; he had to wear the same garment summer and winter; no complaints were tolerated. Indeed there are stories telling how the Spartan boys, would die under the lash of the whip, rather than utter a murmur of complaint.

Women were proud of their sons, and urged them to acts of heroism.

"Return either *with* your shield or *upon* it," they would cry to the young soldiers, going forth to battle.

So the Spartans became a well-trained body of soldiers at a time, when military training was little thought about in Greece. They grew very powerful, and subdued the lesser States around them.

Another important spot in Greece at this time was Athens, and the men of Athens travelled far, to be present at the games of Olympia every four years. They had a lovely city built on a rocky height jutting out into the sea.

There was an old story that the gods Neptune and Athene had a strife as to which should be the patron of the city, and that it was to be given to whichever should produce the most precious gift for it. Neptune struck the earth, and there appeared a war-horse; but Athene's touch brought forth an olive-tree, and this was judged the most useful gift. So the city bore her name, and the olive-tree grew in the court of the old Acropolis, a sacred citadel on a rock above the city.

The King of Athens was called Solon; he was supposed to have been one of the seven wisest men of Greece at this time. He drew up a very clever code of laws for the men of Athens, laws which are spoken of, to the present day.

Corinth was another important centre, from which the Greeks flocked to Olympia. This city stood on the rocky isthmus that connects North and South Greece together; an isthmus called by one of the old poets the "bridge of the untiring sea."

And these three States, Sparta, Athens, and Corinth, played a large part in the history of Greece.

CHAPTER 24

A CLOUD IN THE EAST

"He shall stir up all the realms against Grecia."
—DAN. xi.

WHILE the Greeks were sailing their seas and working out their laws, untroubled by any thoughts of fear, beyond the shores of the blue Mediterranean, great kingdoms were rising and falling in the East.

King Nebuchadnezzar, of whose acts the book of Daniel is so full, had restored the kingdom of Babylon, beyond the Euphrates. He had made the city of Babylon, the greatest city in the world. Stray Greeks had visited it and brought back stories of the amazing palaces and temples, the hanging gardens and terraced parks. With the death of King Nebuchadnezzar the kingdom of Persia rose to fame under King Cyrus.

Now the deeds of Nebuchadnezzar had not troubled Greece at all, but now that Cyrus was King of Persia, things were different. Already Babylon had fallen to him, and he was casting his eyes towards the Greek colonies, on the shores of Asia Minor under one Crœsus.

A story is told of these two monarchs. Cyrus had determined to put Crœsus to death; so he built a great pyre, and placed Crœsus on it, bound in chains. While he stood waiting for the flames to rise around him, some words uttered by Solon, came into his head, and groaning aloud he cried, "Oh, Solon, Solon, Solon!"

Cyrus heard him, and asked of whom he spoke. Crœsus quoted Solon's wise words, "Call no man happy, till his death."

Cyrus was greatly struck. "Surely," he reflected, "here is a man worth saving." And he ordered the prisoner to be set free. But already, the flames were blazing with such strength and fury, that the men could not put them out. Then Crœsus cried to one of the Greek gods for help, and the story says, suddenly clouds came into the clear sky and a downpour of rain put out the roaring fire. So Crœsus lived and became the friend and adviser of the King of Persia.

Under Cambyses, the son of Cyrus, Persia became yet more powerful, for he conquered Egypt from the Pharaohs, and, as we have already seen, would have taken Carthage, if the Phœnician sailors had helped him.

But it was the third great King of Persia, Darius, that the Greeks feared the most, and they had good reason to fear; for was he not king of the mightiest kingdom of the East?

Had not the Persians already subdued the sea-coast on the farther shores of the Archipelago? was not the land of Egypt—that rich and fertile land— theirs too? Was it likely that Darius would be content with what he had, when he could command the soldiers of so many lands?

No sooner had he set his kingdom in order at home, than he started forth on his conquests.

Now when Darius made up his mind to go into Europe, his shortest way would have been to cross the Black Sea; but this was impossible in early days. To get to Europe at all, the water must be crossed, so Darius ordered the Ionian Greeks living on the coast and in the islands off the coast, to raise a fleet of six hundred ships. Then he marched to the shores of the Bosphorus, a narrow strait that divides Asia from Europe. Here a bridge of boats had been made by an engineer from one of the Greek islands belonging to Persia, and the Persian army marched over it to the shores of Europe.

Darius marched the army northward till he reached the river Danube, which, at this time, was supposed to be the greatest river in the world. Here, according to their orders, the Greeks had already built a bridge of boats, across the river. Darius now took a cord—so says the old legend—in which he tied sixty knots.

"Untie one of these knots every day," he said to the Greek captains, "and remain here and guard the bridge till they are all untied. If I have not returned at the end of that time, sail home."

The sixty days passed, the knots were untied, but Darius did not return. The Greeks heard rumours, that the Persians had been defeated and were in full retreat, and that their only hope of safety lay in the bridge.

"Let us destroy the bridge," urged one of the Greeks, Miltiades, the future hero of Marathon; "then shall Darius and his army perish and we shall regain our freedom."

"No," said another; "by destroying Darius, we destroy ourselves."

His counsel prevailed. The Greeks kept the bridge, and Darius passed back in safety.

CHAPTER 25

THE BATTLE OF MARATHON

"The mountains look on Marathon,
And Marathon looks on the sea."
—BYRON.

Now the Ionian Greeks longed for freedom from the Persians. They liked to think they belonged to the mother country, not to these foreigners, whom they had to serve. So they made another attempt to throw off the yoke of Persia, and this time the men of Athens helped them.

But it was no use, for the Persians were too strong for them. Miletus was the strongest of these coast cities belonging to the Ionian Greeks. When the men of Miletus found that the whole great Persian army was about to blockade their city, they resolved, in their despair, to take to their ships and surround the city themselves, and so prevent the Persians entering it. They mustered some three hundred and fifty-three ships in all, but what was their dismay to find, that the Persians had brought double that number, manned by Phœnician sailors!

Then arose a Greek, named Dionysius, commander of the Greek ships. He promised them certain victory, even, over the Phœnician sailors, if they would only work hard under his directions, and learn better how to manage their ships. From morning to night, through seven long summer days, the Greeks practised, under their commander, for the coming battle. But on the eighth day they lost all patience. They were a pleasure-loving race and not used to discipline. They had not been brought up like the Spartan boys. So they left their ships and spent the precious hours, in careless ease, under the shade of the trees on shore.

The Persian fleet attacked, the Greeks scrambled on board; the last struggle for the freedom of Ionia was at hand. But a disgraceful scene followed; many of the Greek ships deserted, and the result was, the capture of Miletus, by the Persians. They killed all the men and carried the women and children into captivity. Everywhere they carried fire and sword, and the Ionian Greeks were more than ever subject to them.

Still Darius was not satisfied. He was very angry with the men of Athens for helping the Ionian Greeks against him, and he made a vow that he would punish them. It is said, that he bade one of his slaves, to say to him three times at dinner, "Sire, remember the Athenians."

It was early, on one September day, in the year 490 B.C., that a great Persian fleet sailed into the Bay of Marathon, the seaport of Athens, in order to attack the city by land and sea. From the heights above the town, the men of Athens beheld the plain crowded with Persian tents, and the bay full of Persian ships—beheld them with terror and awe. Was not this Darius, who had captured their rich seaboard cities in Asia Minor, who possessed Egypt and would fain possess the rest of the world? The very name of Persia was a terror to the Greeks.

A great question was before the men of Athens. Should they await the approach of the great Persian army, or should they boldly go forth to meet them? There were five times as many Persians as Athenians; a fact which seemed to promise no chance of victory. They assembled together. Miltiades spoke. He was the man who had urged the Ionians to destroy the bridge over the Danube some years before. He now proposed that the army should march to Marathon and meet the Persians there. His decision carried the day. He had won undying fame.

The Athenians marched out of their city and encamped on the hills, overlooking the plain of Marathon, for Marathon lay between the mountains and the sea. They were alone in their desperate peril, for the Spartans could hardly arrive in time.

The battle-signal was given, and the whole Greek army, shouting their war-cry, "Io pæan! Io pæan!" charged down the hills, at a run, into the plain of Marathon. Such courage deserved success. For some time Athenians and Persians fought together at Marathon; then the Persians gave way and ran backwards toward the sea, while six thousand lay dead upon the plain.

Thus Athens saved Greece from the Persians. The battle of Marathon was one of the most splendid battles that has ever been fought and won; for had Greece become subject to Darius, the great monarch of the East, the history of Europe might have been, like the history of Asia, a story of misery and oppression.

And still the ships of to-day, sailing eastwards, may see the monument, put up to the heroes of Marathon, bearing the words of the old Greek poet—

"At Marathon for Greece the Athenians fought."

CHAPTER 26

KING AHASUERUS

"This is Ahasuerus which reigned from India even unto Ethiopia, over an hundred and seven and twenty provinces."

—ESTHER i.

WHEN King Darius heard tidings of the defeat of his army at Marathon, he was yet more angry with the Athenians, and more determined than ever to make war against Greece. But before he could get ready again, to march against them, he died, and his son Xerxes became King of Persia. This Xerxes was probably the same king of whom we read, in the Book of Esther, and the great feast that he held in his palace, three years after his father's death, was to arrange about carrying on the war against Greece.

It was not till five years had passed away, that Xerxes was ready to start for Greece, with his enormous army. First of all he ordered a fleet of ships to anchor near Mount Athos, for he remembered the terrible storm, that had wrecked the first Persian expedition to Greece, at this dangerous spot. He made the men from these ships dig a great trench, wide enough for two ships of war to pass side by side, so there was no more danger of shipwreck at Mount Athos.

When all was ready Xerxes himself, came from his palace at Shushan, to review his troops, and to have bridges built over the Hellespont. This was done by Phœnician and Egyptian engineers. But when the work was finished, there arose a great storm, and the bridges were destroyed. Xerxes was very angry at this accident, and not only did he order the engineers to be beheaded, but commanded that three hundred lashes of the whip, should be inflicted on the waters of the Hellespont. Those who scourged the sea were ordered to address it in these words:—

"O bitter water, our lord lays this punishment upon thee for having done him wrong, who never did wrong to thee. King Xerxes will cross thee whether thou wilt or not, thou treacherous and briny river."

Then other engineers set to work and the bridges were made, but they were not finished till the winter had set in.

It was one day, in the early spring, when the sun had but just risen, that the huge army began to cross the bridges, leading them from Asia into Europe. The soldiers and horsemen went over one bridge, while the servants of the army and beasts of burden, went over the other, all crossing under the lash. For this mighty Xerxes was a cruel man. There is a story told of how, just before the crossing of the bridges, an old man came to him and asked him a favour.

"O my lord," said the old man, "I have five sons, and thou art taking them all with thee for this war, which thou makest against the Greeks. Have pity on me, O king, remembering my old age, and release from this service, one of my sons, even the eldest, that he may stay and take care of me."

But the king was furious.

"The life of him whom thou lovest above the rest shall be forfeit," he cried in anger, as he ordered the eldest son to be slain at once. One-half of his body was to be placed on the right side of the road, the other on the left, and the army was ordered to pass between the two halves. Such a man, then, was this great Eastern king, who now hoped to win Europe for himself.

On a marble throne erected on the shore, Xerxes watched his army which, according to old stories, took seven days and seven nights to reach the opposite shore.

While the great fleet lay on the quiet blue waters under the lee of the land, the king held a great review of troops, which showed him to have no less than five million of men under him—the largest number, ever known in ancient or modern history.

There were the Persians, wearing coats of mail and trousers, with their wicker shields, large bows, and short spears. There were men from Assyria with helmets of brass, wooden clubs with knots of iron, and short swords. There were Indians clad in cotton; men from the Caspian shores in goat-skin; men from Ethiopia in Lower Egypt in lion-skins and leopard-skins, armed with arrows, and many others.

King Xerxes looked on his splendid army,—on the glittering helmets, on the countless spears, each with a golden pomegranate at the end; at the eight milk-white horses, that drew the sacred chariot of the god Zeus; at the sea covered with his ships, the land covered with his men,—and he counted himself a happy man.

"But afterwards," says the old historian, "afterwards he wept."

CHAPTER 27

HOW LEONIDAS KEPT THE PASS

"The graves of those who cannot die."
—BYRON.

MEANWHILE, what were the Greeks doing, to prepare for the Persian invasion? There was at Athens, a certain man, but newly risen into the front rank of the citizens. His name was Themistocles. His idea was to make Athens a sea-state, the strongest sea-state in Greece, if possible. He looked out on the bays and inlets of the coast and realised what good harbours they were. He looked beyond, to the many islands, lying in the Archipelago, all offering shelter and refuge to ships, and he saw that one strong fleet, might protect Greece from the Persians, better than any army she could raise.

A rich bed of silver had just been found in the neighbourhood, and the treasury was very rich; so Themistocles advised the Athenians to spend this sum of money, in building new ships, and at last he persuaded them to listen to him. Before many years had passed, Athens had a fleet of two hundred ships—the most powerful fleet in Greece.

Themistocles had some difficulty in carrying his point, because there was another citizen in Athens, who disapproved of his plan. His name was Aristides, and he was known as the Just, because he was the soul of honour. He thought, that if Athens had beaten the Persians once by land, she might do so again. He thought it was better for the people to improve their army, rather than their navy. For his opposition, he was exiled for ten years from Greece, but he found a way of helping Athens afterwards, which has made his name famous.

It was agreed that the King of Sparta should undertake the defence of a narrow pass which connected North and South Greece together, and through which the Persian army must pass.

The name of Leonidas, King of Sparta, will ever live in the world's history for his splendid, if hopeless, defence of the Pass of Thermopylæ. With some hundreds of Spartans he marched northwards, to take up the post allotted to him. The pass lay between high mountains and the sea. It was about a mile long. The narrow entrances were known as the Pylæ or Gates, and the whole pass, distinguished for its hot springs, was known as the Pass of the Hot-Gates. The fleet under a Spartan commander, took up its position at the sea end of the pass; the mountain road was kept by some Greeks from a neighbouring state.

The Persians approached. For four days they lay before the pass without attacking, astonished to see the Spartans quietly practising their gymnastics and combing their long hair, as they did before a festival.

"You will not be able to see the sun for the clouds of javelins and arrows," the Persians cried to Leonidas, before they began the attack.

"We will fight in the shade then," was his quiet and heroic reply.

On the fifth day the Persians attacked, but they met with no success, against the stout-hearted Spartans. Even the choicest of the Persian soldiers, known as the Ten Thousand or the Immortals, made no impression on them.

"Thrice," says the old historian, "the king sprang from his throne in agony for his army."

On the third day after the fighting had begun, a native of Greece told Xerxes of a path over the mountain, and at nightfall a strong Persian force was sent to ascend the path and attack the Greeks in the rear. In the early morning the Greeks, at the head of the pass, heard a trampling through the woods. They fled away in terror and the Persians marched on, behind Leonidas.

In the course of the night, Leonidas knew what had happened. He saw that, if he did not retreat at once, he must be surrounded and perish. But the law of Sparta forbade the soldier to leave his post. Leonidas had no fear of death. The other troops went away, but the King of Sparta and his six hundred men resolved to die at their post. The Persians came on, and things became more and more desperate for the Greeks. Leonidas was killed, and one by one the brave Spartans fell around him.

They did not die in vain. It was a moment when the hearts of the Greeks were wavering and men were inclined to forsake country for self, that the Spartan King Leonidas and his Spartan subjects, showed Greece how citizens should do their duty.

At the entrance to the pass the king and his warriors were buried, while these words were engraved in their memory:—

> "Go, tell the Spartans, thou that passest by,
> That here, obedient to their laws, we lie."

CHAPTER 28

VICTORY FOR THE GREEKS

"A king sat on the rocky brow
Which looks o'er sea-born Salamis:
And ships, by thousands, lay below,
And men in nations:—all were his.
He counted them at break of day—
And when the sun set, where were they?"
—BYRON.

HAVING gained the pass, it was natural that Xerxes should lead his army on to Athens. The Spartans did not care, whether Athens fell into the hands of the Persians, or not. They wished to save Corinth, and so save South Greece, where lay their own land; for Greece was not a united country; each little state wanted what it could get for itself.

The men of Athens knew it was hopeless to try and defend their city alone, against the whole Persian army, so they resolved to abandon it. Very full of sorrow, men, women, and children left their homes and streamed down to the sea-shore, carrying what they could with them. There they found the Greek ships waiting to bear them away, and so when Xerxes and his mighty army reached Athens, they found it silent and deserted. Only a few poor and desperate men had refused to depart, and had posted themselves on the top of the Acropolis, the fortress of Athens. The Persians, disappointed of their prey, took their revenge. They stormed the Acropolis, slew the brave defenders, and set the town on fire.

Athens had fallen. There was but one hope now for the Greeks. They had their ships. Themistocles had been right after all. The ships were yet to save the country.

When Xerxes had advanced to Athens, his fleet had sailed along the coast, and was now anchored. The Greek fleet lay but a few miles off, close to the large island of Salamis, between Athens on the one side and Corinth on the other.

A council of Greeks was held. Themistocles rose to speak at once and to urge a naval battle without delay. The Corinthian general was very angry.

"O Themistocles," he cried, "those who stand up too soon in the games, are whipped."

"Yes," answered Themistocles, "but those who start late, are not crowned."

He saw that the Greeks must fight at once, or in their despair at the loss of Athens, they might not remain faithful. Still he could not get others to see things from his point of view, so he thought of a plan to bring on the battle quickly. He sent a trusty slave across the narrow strait to the Persian admiral, saying that the Greeks were panic-stricken and about to escape. The Persian admiral fell into the trap. In the dead of night, he moved his fleet noiselessly round and blocked up the narrow inlet of the strait, so that the Greeks could not escape.

Early next morning—it was still dark, and the commanders were sitting at council, when Themistocles was called out by a stranger. It was the exile Aristides. In the ruin and distress of Athens, he had come to serve those, who had banished him, and had made his way through the Persian fleet in the darkness, to tell the Greek commanders, that they had been surrounded.

"Themistocles," he urged, "let us still be rivals, but let our contest be, who best shall serve our country."

As the rising sun of the September morning cast its shadows across the blue Bay of Salamis, the Greek fleet put out from shore, to the accustomed notes of the war hymn to Apollo. The enemy's ships faced them all across the narrow strait, stretching far away to right and left, and cutting off all chance of escape. Behind the Persian ships the Persian army was drawn up along the shore, and a lofty throne was set in the midst, from which the great King Xerxes could survey the battle. The Persian fleet advanced, and the Greeks, seized with terror, began to back their oars towards the shore.

Soon the two fleets were engaged. The Greeks fought in good order and kept their ships in line, while the Persian fleet was soon in confusion, oars and helms were broken, ships lay helpless on the water. The old vessels had no rudders, but were steered with broad blades. Confusion soon became a panic. Vessel crashed against vessel. Persian ships were jammed together in the narrow space. Beaten and disabled, they disappeared under the very eyes of Xerxes the king. Some two hundred were thus destroyed, and the rest fled out of the narrow strait. By sunset the battle was over. The Greeks had won their victory and saved their country from the Persians.

And so the great conflict between Eastern tyranny and European freedom was over. Marathon, Thermopylæ, Salamis close one of the most important and thrilling chapters in the world's great history.

CHAPTER 29

SOME GREEK COLONIES

"Hear, for thy children speak, from the uttermost
parts of the sea."
—KIPLING.

Now, while Greece was settling down after her
warfare with Persia, let us take a glance at her
possessions abroad and see how her children over
the seas are getting on.

One of her largest and most important
colonies was Cyrene, on the north coast of Africa,
and opposite the southern point of Greece. It was
one of the fairest spots on the face of the earth.
Standing about ten miles from the sea, high above
sea-level, it was sheltered from the hot blasts of the
desert and open to the cool breezes of the
Mediterranean, over whose blue waters it
commanded a glorious view. Terraces—rich and
fertile—stretched from mountain to shore. To the
west her boundaries reached those of Carthage,
being marked by the "Altar of the Philæni."

A curious story is told of how the men of
Carthage and the men of Cyrene agreed on their

113

boundary. Carthage belonged to the Phœnicians and
Cyrene to the Greeks, and these were rival Powers
on the shores of the Mediterranean.

It was arranged that at a given time two men
from each city should start, and the spot where they
met, should be the boundary. The men of Carthage
chose two brothers called the Philæni. They ran
much faster than the Greeks of Cyrene, so that the
Greeks accused them of starting before the
appointed time. After some dispute the Greeks
agreed to accept the spot as boundary, if the Philæni
would consent to be buried alive, at this very spot in
the sand. The brothers bravely agreed, for their
country's sake, to suffer death; they were accordingly
buried alive in the sand, in the full vigour of their
manhood. Their grateful countrymen erected the
altar to their memory. It was known as the Altar of
the Philæni.

But still more important than Cyrene, was the
Greek colony of Syracuse, the capital of Sicily—the
old legendary land of the Cyclops—known to the
ancients, as Greater Greece.

The great haven of Syracuse, with its island
and its hill, occupied the most striking site on the
east coast of Sicily, and could not fail to invite early
colonists. So, three hundred years before this, the
Greeks had driven out the Phœnicians, who had a
station there, and now it was one of their most
thriving colonies. Like the colonists at Cyrene, the
"lord" of Syracuse sent his racehorses and chariots
to contend in the great games at Olympia, and the

Grecian poets wrote odes in honour of Sicilian victories. Possessing such a fine harbour, this colony of Syracuse had her own ships.

Let us see what these ships were like at this time. The early Greek warships were long and narrow, with twenty-five benches, on each of which sat two oarsmen,—that is to say, they were rowed by no less than fifty oars. Later the Greeks built their ships with two rows of benches, one above the other, so that the number of oarsmen and the speed could be increased without adding to the length of the ship.

But about this time the Phœnicians invented a new sort of ship, and the Greeks soon copied them. The new ship had three banks of oars, and was rowed by no less than one hundred and seventy men. This was the kind of ship that was used by the Greeks at the battle of Salamis. These "triremes," as they were called, had a square sail to be raised when the wind was favourable. Now the men of Syracuse invented an improvement to these triremes as warships. The old idea in naval warfare was to dash the pointed beak of the ship's front into the enemy's vessel, so cutting it in two and causing it to sink. The men of Syracuse made their beaks, or prows, of bronze, which was more effective, and it gave them the victory over the Phœnicians in the harbour of Syracuse.

CHAPTER 30

ACROSS THE BLUE WATERS

"Without freedom, what wert thou, Greece?
Without thee, Greece, what were the world?"
—MÜLLER.

JUST across the blue Mediterranean from Sicily, lay the flourishing colony of Carthage, belonging to the Phœnicians. Now there was great rivalry between these two people, for each owned large possessions along the shores of the Great Sea, and the men of Carthage were known to covet the rich colony of Sicily. It lay but fifty miles across that tideless blue sea, an easy enough voyage for the clever Phœnicians. At last they saw their chance of attacking the Greeks there.

Xerxes, the great King of Persia, was attacking the mother country, Phœnician sailors were manning her ships; was not this the time for the sailors of younger Phœnicia—even the men of Carthage—to sail across and take the younger Greece—even Sicily?

The men of Carthage began to prepare under their commander, Hamilcar. When all was ready they set sail with three thousand ships and an enormous number of men. They had men from the island of Sardinia, from the island of Corsica, and men from Spain; but on the way over, they encountered a terrific storm and a number of ships and horses were lost.

Hamilcar landed at Palermo, at the western end of the three-cornered island.

"The war is over," he murmured as he stepped on shore, so sure did he feel that he would win.

Here he gave his army a rest and then marched on Himera. There he dragged his ships on shore and made a deep ditch to protect them.

A long and terrible battle was fought, in which the men of Carthage were hopelessly defeated, and the Carthaginians went home and told a grand story of the death of their commander.

"All day long," they said, "Hamilcar stood apart from the fight, like Moses of old. All day—for the battle raged from sunrise to sunset—he threw burnt-offerings into a great fire, according to the belief of his forefathers. Towards evening the news reached him, that his army was defeated. The moment for the greatest sacrifice of all had come. And Hamilcar threw himself into the burning fire as the most costly gift of all."

The rest of the story is equally tragic. Another storm overtook the returning fleet, and one little boat alone carried back to Carthage the dismal news that its army, fleet, and commander had perished.

The battle of Himera was fought on the same day as the battle of Salamis, and on both occasions the Greeks were victorious. They had fought bravely for their freedom, they had thrown off the yoke of Persia and the yoke of Carthage.

We must see now what use Greece made of her liberty, and how she taught the world that commerce and trade were not the only ends in view, that ambition in itself was paltry, and how she created that beauty and art, which have influenced nation upon nation, and which play so large a part in the civilisation of to-day.

CHAPTER 31

THE BEAUTY OF ATHENS

"As the flowers adorn the earth and the stars the sky,
so Athens adorns Greece and Greece the world."
—HERDER.

ATHENS and Sparta were now the greatest Powers in Greece, and all the smaller Powers were anxious to obtain the friendship of one or the other. Let us see how Athens outstripped them all. First she sprang into a great commercial city thronged with traders; her merchant ships were in every part of Greece; her navy was the strongest in the world. She had untold wealth, and might have exceeded the old towns of Tyre and Carthage in the glory of her trade.

But one citizen arose, who dreamt of higher things for Greece. His name was Pericles. He saw at once that, since the Persian wars, everything was changed, and he wanted to see the men of Greece capable of ruling themselves and their country. And so while Sparta remained a plain village, Athens became a most beautiful city, which stood forth as an example to others.

Pericles had realised that mere wealth and prosperity alone could never make lasting greatness. He wanted to see his fellow-countrymen happy and prosperous, but he saw this could only come through education. He must wake up the faculties of the Greeks, by making their daily life bright and active, instead of dull and listless.

Under his guidance the temples and statues of the gods were made grand and calm and beautiful. Pictures were painted in public places of the great events in Grecian history, so that the minds of the citizens should dwell on great and noble deeds of heroism, rather than ideas of gaining wealth for wealth's own sake, as the Phœnicians had done before them. Plays, too, were written by great poets, and performed at the cost of the State in a large open building before crowds of people.

These plays were known as tragedies and comedies; they gave the Athenians great pleasure, helping them to enjoy the higher and nobler views of life, rather than the stupid amusements of the day. The great writer of tragedies for the men of Greece was called Æschylus; he had borne shield and spear at Marathon, he had fought at Salamis, and so could write of the Persian wars from his own knowledge.

Sophocles, another great writer, was only fifteen at the battle of Salamis, but he was so beautiful and musical that he was chosen to lead the chorus, which sang the hymn of victory after the battle.

So Athens herself was made beautiful by the wise Pericles. The first spoils of the Persian war had already been devoted to the honour of the goddess of Athens—Athene on the Acropolis. This colossal bronze statue stood warlike and erect, with helmet, spear, and shield, high above the city. And the sailor from afar at sea, could see the point of her spear and the crest of her helmet gleaming across the blue waters. But the goddess Athene was to receive greater honours yet. On the south side of the Acropolis a magnificent temple, known to-day as the Parthenon, was built in her honour, as a storehouse of sacred treasure.

There is an old story which says, that the question was raised, whether the figure should be of marble or of ivory; the great sculptor Phidias suggested marble as the cheapest, but the whole assembly of Athenians shouted aloud for ivory and gold, nothing being too rich for the statue of Athene.

A theatre of music was also built, its pointed roof, made from the masts of the Persian ships which were captured at Salamis, being shaped like the tents of Xerxes.

It was little wonder, then, that when Pericles lay dying, the men of Athens began to talk of the noble deeds he had done, to praise his wisdom, his learning, as well as his buildings.

"He found Athens of brick," they said, "and left her of marble."

Suddenly the sick man raised himself on his bed.

"I wonder," he said, "you praise these things in me, and yet you have left out what is my chief honour—namely, that I never caused any fellow-citizen to put on mourning."

It was perhaps the first time in history, that humanity had been placed above all else.

Such, briefly, was Athens after the Persian wars, unequalled in beauty, unrivalled as queen of Greece.

Phœnicia had given to her colonies the heritage of commerce and trade. Greece gave her colonies a higher heritage than this. Wealth to her was a means to an end; she made her city beautiful, and so raised the minds of her citizens to care for things above riches alone. And this idea grew and spread beyond her city, beyond her colonies, even beyond her empire.

Her poetry has inspired poets of the ages that followed; her historian, Herodotus, is still called the "Father of all history"; her Art alone reached the standard of perfect beauty. What, if the very cause of her greatest glory, was likewise the cause of her fall? She gave to the world that, which no nation had given yet, that, which has helped men to do and die for their country, that which has shown them, that there are higher and better things to live for, than the attainment of wealth or the ambition of conquest.

CHAPTER 32

THE DEATH OF SOCRATES

"And because right is right, to follow right
Were wisdom, in the scorn of consequence."
—TENNYSON.

ONE of the most familiar figures in Athens at this time was that of Socrates, and the story of his life and death, thrills us with interest to-day. His youth and manhood were passed in the most splendid period of Athenian history. Pericles was making the city beautiful; men were writing poetry and history, as they had never been written since the world began; art and sculpture ranked high in that period of genius. As a boy, Socrates received the usual education in music and gymnastics; he learnt a little science and mathematics, and understood something of astronomy.

But his greatness did not spring from his learning, rather it sprang from his thoughtfulness, and his close observation of his fellow-men. He was a man who hated everything sham, or hollow. He loved truth and justice for their own sake; he loved all that was high, and honourable, and right. He was a well-known figure in Athens, for all day long, he wandered about the streets, now talking with a group of clever men at one of the corners, now speaking to the children, who might care to listen, now arguing with his devoted pupils and disciples.

This great Socrates was strange enough to look at. He was very ugly, with a flat nose and prominent eyes, and he was dressed very shabbily, because he was always poor. When the men of Athens turned on him at the last, and brought him up for trial, £4 was all he had to offer for his life. Wealth, beauty, praise,—these things he despised as unworthy. Truth, justice, courage, honour,—these were the things, that made a man acceptable to his God.

Here is the account of him by his great friend. "At one time we were fellow-soldiers together," he says. "His fortitude in enduring cold was surprising. There was a severe frost, for the winter in that region is really tremendous; and everybody else either remained indoors, or if they went out, had on an amazing quantity of clothes, and were well shod and had their feet swathed in felt and fleeces; in the midst of this, Socrates, with his bare feet on the ice and in his ordinary dress, marched better than the other soldiers who had shoes, and they looked daggers at him because he seemed to despise them."

Such was the man who stood head and shoulders above his fellows. Let us look at him when he is an old man still discoursing, in the streets of Athens. This time he is speaking to two little

"Socrates was a well-known figure in Athens."

schoolboys on friendship. He has just been brought into a newly built school.

"Having come in," he says, "we found the boys all in their white array, and games at dice were going on among them. There was also a circle of lookers-on: among them was Lysis. He was standing with the other boys and youths, having a crown upon his head, like a vision, and not less worthy of praise for his goodness than for his beauty. We went over to the opposite side of the room, where we sat down and began to talk. This attracted Lysis, who was constantly turning round to look at us—he was evidently wanting to come to us."

Presently Lysis and a boy friend came and sat down by the old man, and Socrates began talking to them.

"Which of you two youths is the elder?" he asked.

"That is a matter of dispute between us," answered one of the boys.

"And which is the nobler? Is that also a matter of dispute?"

"Yes, certainly," they answered.

"And another disputed point is, which is the fairer?"

The two boys laughed.

"I do not ask which is the richer of the two," he said, "for you are friends, are you not?"

"Certainly," they replied.

"And friends have all things in common, so that one of you can be no richer than the other, if you say truly that you are friends."

In this way the wise old man talked to the boys. But as time went on, the men of Athens did not approve of his teaching. He talked as if there were higher things than sacrificing to the Greek gods, and the Greeks grew alarmed.

The trial and death of Socrates, as it has been written by his beloved pupil Plato, is one of the masterpieces even to-day in the world's history. He tells, how Socrates appeared before his judges, the men of Athens, to answer the charges against himself, and it gives the words of that wonderful defence. Socrates begs for his life, not for his own sake, but for theirs: he is their heaven-sent friend, though they know it not. He is an old man already, and the Athenians will gain nothing by taking away from him the few years of life remaining. But they can acquit him or condemn him, he is willing to die many deaths for the cause he feels to be right.

And the men of Athens condemned him to die.

Fearlessly he speaks to his judges of death.

"Be of good cheer about death," he cries to the crowded court, "and know of a certainty that no evil can happen to a good man, either in life, or after death. The hour of departure has arrived and we go our ways—I to die and you to live. Which is better, God only knows."

Every touching detail of the last hours of the master is carefully told by his faithful pupil Plato.

The sun was just setting upon the hills behind Athens, when Socrates took the cup of poison, which was to end his seventy years of work. Friend after friend broke down, and sobs of strong men filled the room as the Greek philosopher lay dying.

"What is this strange outcry?" he asked at last. "I have been told that a man should die in peace. Be quiet, then, and have patience."

And so he died, "of all the men of his time, the wisest and justest and best."

CHAPTER 33

RETREAT OF THE TEN THOUSAND

"A march in the ranks hard-pressed and the road unknown."
—W. WHITMAN.

SOCRATES was dead, and the brilliant period, which had made Athens the mistress of Greece, was dead too. Pericles had foreseen truly that sooner or later there must be war between Athens and Sparta. It was well for him that he died before the result of that war was known; for the fall of his beautiful city, which took place during the lifetime of Socrates, would have broken his heart. After a long war the Spartans took formal possession of Athens; but to accomplish this, they had called in the help of the Persians.

And so it came to pass, when the Persians wanted help, they called in the help of the Spartan Greeks. It is a wonderful story, how ten thousand Greeks marched into the very heart of the Persian empire, and a yet more wonderful one of their retreat.

The expedition started two years before the death of Socrates. It was led by Cyrus, the younger brother of the reigning King of Persia, who wished to make himself king instead. But the true object of the expedition was kept secret from the Greek soldiers.

Marching inland through Asia Minor, they skirted the north of Phœnicia and marched on till they reached the river Euphrates. Here it was impossible to keep from the Greeks, the secret, that they were indeed marching against the King of Persia. To the complaining army, which had been so deceived, Cyrus was full of promises. Each soldier should receive a year's pay, and "to each of you Greeks, moreover," added Cyrus, "I shall present a wreath of gold."

This speech impressed the Greeks favourably, and they agreed to go on. They now plunged into the desert, "smooth as a sea, treeless," but alive with all kinds of beasts strange to the Greek eyes—wild asses, ostriches, and antelopes. For thirteen days they tramped through the desert, until they reached the edge of the land of Babylon.

And now they learned that the king's host was advancing. It was not long before the two armies were engaged in battle. But though the King of Persia was well prepared, and had a strong force of Egyptians to help him, the Greeks won the victory. The Persians were flying before them, when suddenly Cyrus caught sight of his brother,—the brother whom he hated with his whole soul. He galloped forward, hoping to slay him with his own hand. He got near enough to throw his javelin and wound him, but in the scuffle that ensued Cyrus was slain.

The Greeks were now in the heart of Persia, girt about by foes on every side—their leader dead, their cause destroyed. Their one great desire was to get home. But they had no food, and they did not know the way. The king now pretended he would send a guide who would take them safely back to their own country; but treachery was at work, and the Greeks were deserted when they were yet eight months' march, by the shortest way from home. Rivers and desert land lay before them; Persian troops were waiting to fall on them. They were in despair. Few ate any supper that night; every man lay down to rest, but not to sleep, for they were heavy with sorrow, and longing for those they might never see again.

Amid the ranks was a young Athenian called Xenophon. He had been a pupil of Socrates. That night he had a dream which made him spring up at dawn.

"Why am I lying here?" he cried to himself. "At daybreak the enemy will be upon us and we shall be killed."

He called the officers together; he urged immediate action. His speech put new life into the despairing men; they swore to obey him, and so began one of the most wonderful marches the world has ever seen. They went on till they came to the mountains, where dwelt some wild tribes, who stood on steep heights shooting arrows and throwing down stones at them. After much suffering and loss of life, they reached Armenia. It was December, and their way home lay through wintry snows and ice. On and on plodded the Ten Thousand; cold and hunger was their lot, but home lay before them, and encouraged by their young leader Xenophon, they would reach Greece yet.

Suddenly, one day, a great cry arose from those in front. Xenophon, who was behind with the rear, galloped up quickly, fearing an enemy. As fresh men galloped to the front, the cry increased.

"The sea! the sea!" cried the Greeks, as they reached the summit of a hill and saw in the distance the blue waters. The sight of the sea was to the weary men, as the sight of home. Their troubles would soon be over now, and they wept on each other's necks for very joy. It was only the Black Sea, and they had many long miles yet to march.

Now that the danger of attack was over, the army began to loose its strength of union, and Xenophon had all he could do to keep it together.

Notwithstanding Xenophon's entreaties, the Ten Thousand, now reduced in numbers, fell away from the brave beginnings. They plundered the country through which they passed, and at last Xenophon handed them over to a Spartan general to take charge of them.

Then Xenophon returned to Athens, and settling in a quiet country place near Olympia, he wrote the account of the Retreat of the Ten Thousand, and it is due to his industry and talent, that we know the famous story of their wonderful march.

CHAPTER 34

THE STORY OF ROMULUS AND REMUS

"The troubled river knew them,
    And smoothed his yellow foam,
And gently rocked the cradle
    That bore the fate of Rome."
        —MACAULAY.

GOING westward from Greece, another peninsula stretches down into the Mediterranean Sea. In shape it is something like a long leg, and at the lower end, lies the island of Sicily, which resembles a foot. We have already heard something of Sicily, and seen how the Greeks had colonies there. There is also the old story of how Æneas escaped from the siege of Troy, carrying on his back his aged father, and how, after years of adventures, he landed on the shores of Italy and built the city of Alba Longa, where for hundreds of years his descendants lived.

At the end of this time—so runs the old legend—there was a king called Numitor. He had a brother, Amulius, who drove him from the throne, slew his daughter, and seized her two baby sons.

134

Amulius then gave orders, that the babies should be thrown into the river Tiber, which flowed through the city. Now the Tiber had overflowed its banks, and when the waters began to subside the cradle containing the twin babies was left high and dry, on the shallow ground, at the foot of the Palatine Hill.

There, says the story, they were found by a shepherd. He was walking by the river, when he saw a cradle lying under a fig-tree, and beside the cradle, stood a large wolf. She had taken care of the children, but now she ran away into the woods and the shepherd carried the babies home to his wife. She named them Romulus and Remus, and brought them up as shepherds.

So in this home at the foot of the Palatine Hill the boys grew to manhood,—they grew also very strong and brave. One day, as years went on, they discovered their origin, that they were the grandsons of Numitor, who had been dethroned by his brother. So the twins arose, collected an army, drove away Amulius, and brought their grandfather back to Alba Longa. They then resolved to build a new city for themselves, on one of the seven low hills, beneath which ran the yellow river Tiber.

But Remus wanted to build on one hill and Romulus on another. Their grandfather advised them each to stand on a hill, and whichever of them saw the greatest number of vultures flying, he should build the city on his chosen hill. Remus saw six vultures, but Romulus saw twelve from the Palatine

Hill, so that was made the beginning of the new city, and Romulus was chosen king.

Yoking together a white cow and a snow-white bull to a ploughshare, he drew a furrow around the Palatine and began to build the walls of the city. But Remus was angry with him, and before the walls had reached his own height he jumped over them, mocking as he did so. He was immediately slain, while Romulus cried, "So perish all who dare to climb these ramparts."

He called the name of the city Rome, after himself, and lived in a mud hovel, covered with thatch in the midst of it.

This was in the year 753, and the Romans count their history from this date, just as the Greeks count theirs from the beginnings of the Olympic games.

Under Romulus the population of the new city grew apace, partly because he allowed it to be a refuge for runaway slaves and murderers. He made laws and appointed a senate—a body of elderly men to help him with the government. It was this Romulus, too, who divided the year into ten months, the first being March, named from Mars, the god he delighted to honour. But his successor added two more, making January the first month, after the god Janus, to whom he had built a temple.

This was how Rome began,—that Rome which was to play such an immense part in the world's great history—Rome, the Eternal City;

Rome, the City of the Seven Hills; Rome, long ago, the Mistress of the World.

CHAPTER 35

HOW HORATIUS KEPT THE BRIDGE

"With weeping and with laughter
Still is the story told,
How well Horatius kept the bridge
In the brave days of old."
—MACAULAY.

STILL in the shadow-land of history, a family called Tarquin came to live in Rome. Their father, a wealthy merchant, had come from Greece, bringing with him some of the artists and sculptors, whose genius had made his Greek home so beautiful. Tarquin married an Italian lady and made great friends with the king, at whose death he became King of Rome himself.

So a Greek ruled over Rome. This Tarquin was the first Roman king to wear a purple robe and crown of gold, and he planned a sort of little Olympia, in the plain below the city, where games could be played and chariot-races run. For over a hundred years, the Tarquins ruled over Rome, and they did a great deal for the city, by introducing what they had learnt in Greece. But after a time the Romans rose against them. They dethroned the last of the Tarquins and elected two consuls instead.

Tarquin fled to a great and powerful king called Lars Porsena, who collected an army and marched with him to Rome to help him regain his lost kingdom. But the Romans had a brave citizen called Horatius, and the legend says he defended the bridge over the Tiber and so saved Rome.

This is the story: While Lars Porsena and his huge army were on the march to Rome, laying waste the country, through which they passed, the consul of Rome and the Fathers of the City were holding a hurried council before the River Gate. "The bridge must be destroyed," said the consul. "Nothing else can save the town."

"Just then a scout came flying,
All wild with haste and fear:
'To arms! to arms! Sir Consul:
Lars Porsena is here.'"

On the low hills to the westward, the great army could be seen. Louder and louder sounded the trumpet's war-notes, while in broken gleams shone the long array of bright helmets and glittering spears. Under the royal standard Lars Porsena himself sat in his ivory car. The Roman consul grew very grave.

" 'Their van will be upon us
Before the bridge goes down;

And if they once may win the bridge,
What hope to save the town?'

Then out spake brave Horatius,
The Captain of the Gate:
'To every man upon this earth
Death cometh soon or late.
And how can man die better
Than facing fearful odds,
For the ashes of his fathers,
And the temples of his Gods.

'Hew down the bridge, Sir Consul,
With all the speed ye may;
I, with two more to help me,
Will hold the foe in play.
In yon strait path a thousand
May well be stopped by three.
Now who will stand on either hand,
And keep the bridge with me!' "

Two Romans stepped forth at once and offered to help, and the dauntless three went forth against the mighty army of Lars Porsena.

"Now while the Three were tightening
Their harness on their backs,
The Consul was the foremost man
To take in hand an axe:
And Fathers, mixed with Commons,
Seized hatchet, bar, and crow,
And smote upon the planks above,
And loosed the props below."

On came the great host, laughing at the thought of three men keeping the bridge against them. Three chiefs with swords and shields came forward to fight, but in a few minutes they all three lay dead at the feet of Horatius and his two friends. Forward came another three, but only to meet with the same fate. The laughter died away, and for a time, none dared venture forth against these brave Romans.

"But meanwhile axe and lever
     Have manfully been plied;
And now the bridge hangs tottering
     Above the boiling tide.
'Come back, come back, Horatius!'
     Loud cried the Fathers all.
'Back, Lartius! back, Herminius!
     Back, ere the ruin fall!'

Back darted Spurius Lartius;
     Herminius darted back:
And, as they passed, beneath their feet
     They felt the timbers crack.
But when they turned their faces,
     And on the farther shore
Saw brave Horatius stand alone,
     They would have crossed once more.

But with a crash like thunder
     Fell every loosened beam,
And, like a dam, the mighty wreck
     Lay right athwart the stream.
And a long shout of triumph
     Rose from the walls of Rome,
As to the highest turret-tops
     Was splashed the yellow foam."

Alone stood Horatius—thrice 30,000 foes before and the broad flood behind. His foes besought him to yield, but he took no notice. He looked beyond the rushing river, to the white porch of his home, on the Palatine Hill, and then he cried to the river that rolls by the towers of Rome—

> " 'Oh, Tiber! father Tiber!
> To whom the Romans pray,
> A Roman's life, a Roman's arms,
> Take thou in charge this day.' "

With these words he plunged headlong into the fiercely flowing river. Not a sound of joy or sorrow rose from either bank. All watched in breathless silence the brave man's struggles. Suddenly they saw his helmet appear above the foaming waters, and a shout of delight arose from the Romans—

> " 'Heaven help him!' quoth Lars Porsena,
> 'And bring him safe to shore;
> For such a gallant feat of arms
> Was never seen before.' "

Horatius reached home in safety, and amid weeping and clapping he was borne through the gate of Rome by the joyous crowds. They erected a golden statue of their hero and wrote his deed in letters of gold.

CHAPTER 36

CORIOLANUS

"O my mother, mother! O
You have won a happy victory to Rome:
But, for your son——"
—SHAKSPERE.

HERE is one more story of the old Roman days, before the true history of Rome begins. It is the story of a man, who became a traitor to his country, which was only saved by his mother's tears.

When Coriolanus was a boy he was called Caius Marcius. His mother brought him up in Rome, to be all that a boy ought to be, brave and honourable and true. He was also strong, and could run so fast, that none could compare with him. He first fought in the battle of Lake Regillus, said to have been won by the twin gods Castor and Pollux on their snow-white steeds. For his bravery he received a crown of oak-leaves, though only sixteen at the time.

There was a tribe of people living some way from Rome who had a quarrel with the Romans. They were known as Volscians. Against one of their towns, called Corioli, the Romans now marched, and among them was the young Caius Marcius. He fought so well, that it was mainly due to him, that the town was taken. Wherever the fight was thickest, there was the young Roman. At last he was badly wounded. The soldiers begged him to go to his tent that his wounds might be dressed, and rest.

"It is not for conquerors to be tired," he cried, and went on fighting.

The fighting over, and the town of Corioli taken, the Roman consul made a speech to the army, praising the gallant deeds of Caius Marcius.

"Of all the plunder we have gained we will give the tenth part to Caius Marcius," he said, "for he has well deserved it."

He then crowned him and gave him the surname of Coriolanus in honour of his victory. Coriolanus refused all reward; he only asked for the freedom of a friend who had been taken prisoner.

Soon after this, there was a great famine in Rome. During the wars, no one had tilled the land, and there was no corn, except what was brought from Sicily.

One day a large shipload of corn arrived from Sicily; Coriolanus stood up in the Senate and proposed withholding it from the people. The people were furious.

"Coriolanus would take from us this foreign corn, which is our only chance of getting bread for our children," they cried, "unless we give up our power of voting for laws. He will make us slaves or force us to die of hunger."

They tried to kill Coriolanus, and the Senate ordered that he should be tried. He was tried and condemned to exile. He must leave Rome and never return.

In vain he pleaded that he loved his country. The people were firm. He must go. Then the love of Coriolanus for Rome turned to hate, and with the fierce words, "There is a world elsewhere," he left them.

He went straight to the country of the Volscians, and entering the house of the warrior chief, he sat down by the fire and covered his face with his cloak. At last he spoke.

"I am Caius Marcius," he said, "the man who has done so much to harm you. The ungrateful people of Rome have driven me away from their city. I come to ask you to let me join you against the Romans."

The warrior was greatly surprised; but the Volscians were delighted to have Coriolanus, and very soon they led a large army against Rome.

When the Romans heard that the banished Coriolanus was in command of an army of the Volscians within five miles of Rome, they were very much alarmed. They sent friends of his—men he once loved—to plead with him for his native city; but Coriolanus told them unless they would give up a large piece of land to the Volscians he would fight.

Again the Romans sent messengers to plead with him. But in vain. He would not relent. He intended to have his revenge on Rome. At last the Romans thought of a last resource. They remembered the love that Coriolanus had always borne his mother, and they now begged her to go to him and beg him to spare Rome.

"You have saved Rome, but lost your son."

Taking one of her little grandsons by the hand, accompanied by her daughter-in-law leading the other, and followed by a band of Roman women, Volumnia stood, one day, before her exiled son Coriolanus. In pitiful terms she told him of Rome's unhappiness at his action; she spoke of her own misery at his fall and plan of revenge; she reminded him of his upright youth, his honour, and his old love for her. Kneeling at his feet, the two women and the children entreated him to spare Rome. The proud man was touched. What the other messengers could not do these Roman women had accomplished.

"Oh mother, mother! what have you done?" he cried, gently raising her up. "You have saved Rome, but lost your son. I go, conquered by you alone."

The women carried the glad news back to Rome, and Coriolanus led his army back to the Volscians. But they were angry at his having made peace with their enemies, and they arose and killed him.

So Coriolanus died, and the Romans built a temple on the spot where Volumnia had knelt to him.

CHAPTER 37

ALEXANDER THE GREAT

"Men are but children of a larger growth."
—DRYDEN.

WHILE Rome is struggling into existence, while Carthage is growing in power on the opposite coast of Africa, let us take a look at a newly growing nation to the north of Greece, which threatened for a time the whole existing world. The story of this nation, which was known as Macedonia, is really the story of Alexander the Great, for it was due to his greatness alone, that Macedonia became the power she was.

Some two hundred miles to the north of Athens, lay the little mountainous country of Macedonia. It was of little or no importance in the then known world, until a king called Philip arose, who in the year 356 B.C. had a son called Alexander. Philip boasted his descent from Hercules, while his wife traced her lineage back to the hero Achilles, so that in the boy Alexander two lines of ancient northern kings were joined.

One story survives of Alexander's boyhood, which shows what stuff he was made of. A vicious horse was one day brought before King Philip in a field where he was standing with his wife and son. But the animal seemed so fierce and unmanageable, rearing high when the grooms tried to mount it, that Philip bade them take it away.

"What an excellent horse they are losing for want of skill and spirit to manage him," said the boy Alexander several times, until his father turned to him, saying, "Young man, you find fault with your elders, as if you could manage the horse better."

"I could manage this horse better than others do," answered the boy.

"And if you do not," said his father, "what will you pay for your rashness?"

"I will pay the whole price of the horse," he answered bravely.

At this the whole company laughed, but Alexander ran at once to the horse. Laying hold of the animal's bridle, he turned him first to the sun, for he noticed how the strong shadow disturbed the animal. Then letting him go forward a little, still keeping the reins in his hand and stroking him gently, when he found him beginning to grow fiery, he let fall his upper garment softly and with one nimble leap, securely mounted him. When he was seated, he drew in the bridle and curbed him gradually, without striking him. Then he let him go at full speed, urging him on with a commanding voice and touching him with his heel.

The king and assembled company looked on, in silent anxiety, till they saw the boy riding the horse back in triumph. Then they all burst out in loud applause, and his father kissed him with tears in his eyes as he cried in his joy, "O my son, look thee out a kingdom equal to thyself, for Macedonia is too small for thee."

Philip now sent for Aristotle, the most learned and celebrated philosopher of his time, to come and teach his son, who was now thirteen. Aristotle had been the pupil of Plato, from whom he must have learnt much of Socrates, Plato's beloved master. Such a man, then, as this Aristotle—whose works are read and taught everywhere today—was likely to train the mind of this exceptional boy to the very best advantage.

A story is told, that Aristotle taught several princes, as well as Alexander, in the school by the shady Grove. One day he said to one of these kings' sons, "When, some day, you become king, what favour do you think you will show me, your teacher?"

"You shall dine at my table, and I will make all show you honour and respect," answered the boy.

"And you?" he inquired of another.

"I will make you my chief treasurer," answered the next.

Then turning to Alexander he said, "And you, my son, what do you propose to do with me, your old teacher, when you come to sit on the throne of your father?"

"What right have you to ask me of the future?" answered the boy. "As I have no knowledge of the morrow, I can only say, that when the day and hour is come, then I will give you your answer."

"Well said," cried his master, "well said, Alexander, world-monarch, for thou wilt one day be the greatest king of all."

And Aristotle was right.

CHAPTER 38

KING OF MACEDONIA

"My son, thou art invincible."
—DELPHIAN ORACLE.

WHEN he was but sixteen years old, Alexander had his first experience of public affairs; for in the summer of this year, 340, Philip set out on an expedition, leaving his young son "in charge of affairs and of the seal." Alexander made better use of his time than his father; for where Philip had failed, his son succeeded beyond all expectation in subduing a restless mountain tribe. His influence now grew rapidly, and the Macedonians murmured already, "Alexander is king."

But a family quarrel arose; hot words passed between Alexander and his father. There was a scene, in which the king sprang on his son with drawn sword; but he fell down before he reached him, and Alexander's taunt has passed into history.

"Here is a man," he cried scornfully, "who has been preparing to cross from Europe into Asia, but he has been upset in crossing from one couch to another."

After this, Alexander and his mother left the country. But not for long. Before the year was out Philip was dead—killed by an assassin—and Alexander was king of Macedonia.

He was surrounded by enemies on all sides. Now, since the days of Socrates, when Athens was at the height of her glory, Greece had suffered greatly from her want of unity. She had been torn by her small wars, and even the common danger of Persia had not brought her union. Now there was another common danger, but the Greeks were slow to realise it. There was one Greek citizen, however, who saw more clearly than the rest, how yearningly the eyes of Philip were turned towards Greece.

"Let the Greeks cease their quarrels with one another and unite to preserve the liberty, which is their birthright, against the despot who seeks to enslave them all."

Such was the cry of Demosthenes, this far-seeing man—the most famous orator Greece ever had. But he cried to the people in vain. Philip came down to Greece, and it was not long before her liberties were crushed and she became a province of Macedonia. Now, Philip was dead, and the Grecian states hoped to shake off the yoke of Macedonia. Demosthenes was seen in the streets of Athens, wearing a garland about his head and dressed in white, as for a holiday, for he knew the enemy of Athens was dead, and he did not know, that Alexander would be a greater conqueror, than his father had been.

The new young King of Macedonia, though full of foreign schemes, first turned his attentions to Greece. He marched south to Corinth. City after city in Greece submitted to the new and powerful King of Macedonia, until with the fall of Thebes, the last Grecian town to hold out, Alexander's campaign in Europe was at an end. The rest of his life was spent in Asia.

The world toward which Alexander had set his face, and which he was now preparing to enter, was the great old world of the East—that world which was great long before Greece and Rome—that world which was being left utterly behind, in the great march of mankind forwards.

The boundary between Asia and Europe has always been a rigid one. It was the same in the days of Alexander as it is to-day. The continents are divided by customs, dress, homes, and faith—differences that thousands of years have never succeeded in altering; for the difference of East and West abides in the very heart of things.

To unite the East and West was the dream of Alexander's life—that is to say, he tried to do what has not been done even to-day. He wanted to conquer the great old world, to teach the men of the East about Greece, to tame the old world and bring it into order. He did not succeed in doing this, but he did succeed in a great deal that he set out to do.

CHAPTER 39

CONQUEST OF THE EAST

"See the conquering hero comes,
Sound the trumpet, beat the drums."
—NATH. LEE, Alexander the Great.

BEFORE starting forth on his great expedition, Alexander divided his royal forests and domains among his friends, as though he expected never to return.

"And what is left for yourself?" asked one of these friends.

"Hope," was the fine answer.

"Then," cried the friend, rejecting his portion of the land, "we who go forth to fight with you need share only in your hope."

Such was the enthusiasm with which Alexander left his country.

The Persian empire was very weak at this time, and governed by a feeble monarch. Two generations had passed away since Xenophon had led his famous Ten Thousand into the heart of the country. Alexander had no doubts as to his being

155

able to conquer it. He soon reached the Hellespont, or, as we now call it, the Dardanelles, and steering with his own hands the flagship across the narrowest spot, where one hundred and forty-six years before, Xerxes had stretched his famous bridge of boats, he was the first to leap ashore. He had already hurled a spear into the soil from the prow of the ship, where, in full armour, he stood. While the mighty Greek army was crossing the narrow water, in the one hundred and sixty triremes hired for the purpose, Alexander was hurrying to Troy, to honour the memory of the heroes, who were buried there, to crown with a garland the gravestone of his forefather Achilles, and to sacrifice to Athena. This episode shows how imbued Alexander was with Greek traditions—indeed, it is said, he always carried with him a copy of Homer's works, so much did he admire the old blind poet of Greece.

Meanwhile the Persian troops were encamped on the farther bank of a little river, and it was necessary to fight in the gate of Asia, as it were, for an entrance. The day was far advanced when Alexander made up his mind to attack. His old general advised him to wait till morning broke to cross the river.

"I should be ashamed," cried the young king, "having crossed the Hellespont, to be detained by this paltry little stream. If I halt now, the Persians will take courage and flatter themselves they are a match for the Macedonians."

Sending on some of his cavalry to engage the enemy, Alexander, in his glittering armour, mounted his horse, called to his men to remember their valour, and while the trumpets blared, and the war-cry echoed far, he plunged into the stream. Showers of arrows fell on them as they struggled through the water, while the Persians hurled javelins down on them from the opposite banks. But at last they gained the muddy bank on the farther shore, and with spears attacked the foe. Alexander was in the thick of the fight, his large plume of white feathers making him ever a marked man; but he gained a splendid victory and escaped without a wound. Some of the Persian rugs and golden goblets—rich booty of his victory—he sent home to his mother; three hundred suits of armour were sent to Athens to be hung up in the Acropolis.

Alexander had now made his name. He was but twenty-two, blue-eyed and golden haired, with a clear white skin, and very beautiful to look on. But, better than all this, he was frank and generous; fear to him was unknown; he was loyal to his friends, and he was greatly beloved.

With the dust of battle still on him he led his army forwards. Ephesus soon fell into his hands, in gratitude for which, he helped to rebuild the great temple of Diana, which had been destroyed the day of his own birth. It was not long before the whole of Asia Minor had fallen into his hands. There is a story told of him, when he was at a place called Gordia, from which the saying "Gordian knot" has been taken. On the hill above the town, stood the royal palace of King Midas, where stood a famous chariot to which the yoke was fastened by the knotted bough of a cornel-tree. It was said that whoever could untie this knot, should be lord of Asia. To the delight of all, Alexander somehow managed to cut the knot and so fulfil the prophecy.

It was spring-time when he dashed down over some high mountains, to take possession of the town of Tarsus. After a long ride in the burning sun he bathed in the cool waters of a stream, which brought on a violent chill, and nearly ended his life. As soon as he was well enough, he dashed onwards, for he knew that a large Persian host was advancing against him. A magnificent host it was. In the centre of it was the king in a high and richly adorned chariot, wearing a purple mantle trimmed with precious stones. He was surrounded by a band of Immortals, in golden robes, carrying silver-handled lances. Following him, in covered chariots, were his mother, his wives and children, six hundred mules and three hundred camels with their luggage.

The Persians made sure of crushing Alexander this time. But it was not to be. Alexander gained another great victory; the Immortals gave way; the king sprang from his chariot, mounted a horse, and never rested till he was on the far side of the river Euphrates. He had left his old mother behind at the mercy of the victor.

Having conquered Asia Minor, Alexander proceeded to Phœnicia and took Tyre after a long siege. Then he went down into Egypt.

158

CHAPTER 40

THE CONQUEST OF INDIA

"Turn, and the world is thine."
—KIPLING.

IT was now two and a half years since Alexander had entered Asia. The fall of Tyre had given him not only Syria, but Egypt too, and the command of the sea, in this part of the Mediterranean. For Egypt was not strong enough to withstand this world-conqueror, so Alexander was crowned king at Memphis, the old capital of the Pharaohs. Here he held athletic games and a contest of poets, to which the most famous artists came over from Greece. From Memphis he sailed down the river Nile and founded a city, which is still called by his name, Alexandria, the port of Egypt. The new lord of Egypt and Syria, with the whole coast-land now in his possession, then started for Persia once more, for the Shah was again preparing to oppose him.

A great battle was fought—one of the greatest on record of the ancient world. The Shah had once more to ride breathlessly for his life, his army was scattered to the winds, and thousands were made captive.

It seemed, indeed, that Alexander was invincible. Babylon submitted to him at once, Shushan, the old capital, fell without a blow, and the victorious monarch marched ever forwards. The death of the Shah of Persia put fresh power into his hands. It was the task of his life to spread Greek ideas in the East: the best way to do this seemed to be, to become king of the East, according to Eastern ideas. So he surrounded himself with Eastern forms and pomp; he married a Persian wife; he dressed in the white tunic, and wore the Persian girdle, common to the great Eastern rulers.

This change was highly unpopular with his countrymen.

One night at a feast in one of the Persian fortresses, Clitus, the foster-brother and dear friend of Alexander, suddenly sprang up and began to abuse the king. They had all been drinking the strong wines of the country, and stung by the taunts of Clitus, Alexander rose. He snatched a spear, and in a sudden fury dashed it into his foster-brother. Clitus sank to the ground—dead. An agony of remorse followed for Alexander; for three days he lay in his tent, neither sleeping nor eating, till at last they roused him.

"Is this the Alexander, whom the whole world looks to, lying here and weeping like a slave?" cried one of his friends, as he beheld the prostrate form of the king.

Alexander now turned his eyes towards India, still to the outer world, an unknown land. Strange stories of its wonders, had reached the Greek invaders—stories of monster ants, who turned up gold-dust from the vast sand deserts; stories of men clothed in garments, made of plaited rushes, like mats; of trees that bore wool, instead of fruit; of lakes full of oil; of giants, dwarfs, and palm-trees that touched the skies.

Alexander and his army crossed the barriers of the Hindu Kush mountains, and entered the plains, through which flowed the river Indus. He had again passed from one world into another, a world which was to remain unknown for twenty centuries after the days of Alexander, until the discovery of the Cape of Good Hope should open out a sea-path to India.

Crossing the Indus by a bridge of boats, he found himself in the district, now known as the Punjab, where five rivers meet. On the opposite bank of one of these rivers a powerful Indian king, named Porus, disputed his advance. A battle was fought, in which the sight and smell of the Indian elephants, on which King Porus's men were mounted, frightened the Persian horses. Finally, however, Alexander won. The vanquished Indian king was brought before him; he was very tall and majestic, and his bravery in battle had excited the admiration of the king. He inquired of Porus how he would wish to be treated.

"As a king," was the stern answer.

"And have you no other request?" asked Alexander.

"No," answered Porus, "everything is included in the word king."

So struck was he with this answer, that Alexander restored him his kingdom.

It was soon after this battle, that Alexander lost his beautiful horse Bucephalus, the one he had tamed as a boy, and which had carried him ever since. The poor beast died of age and weariness, and the king built a city, to its memory, on the banks of the river; which monument survives today—the city of Jalalpur.

Alexander longed to press on, and see all the wonders of India and the great river Ganges, but the Macedonians were weary of the march and absolutely refused to go another step farther. Their clothes were worn out, and they had to wrap their bodies in Indian rags; the hoofs of their horses were rubbed away by the long rough marches; their arms were blunted and broken. And the king, with unexplored lands yet before him, had to turn back.

He reached Babylon in the spring of 324, and at once began to fortify it, as the capital of his new and mighty empire. Here he held his court, seated on the golden throne of the Persians, with a golden canopy studded with emeralds and precious stones. Here he received people from every known country. Here he stood at the highest point of glory, knowing not, how near the end was.

While he was preparing for the conquest of Arabia, he was taken with a violent fever; he lay in bed eagerly discussing details, but he grew rapidly worse. In the cool of one June evening, while the fever was yet raging, they carried him to the river and rowed him across to a garden villa. As he grew worse they took him back to the palace. One by one the Macedonian soldiers filed past the bed of their young and dying king; he was too ill to speak to them. A few days later, Alexander the Great lay dead at the early age of thirty-three.

Into thirteen years he had compressed the energies of a lifetime, for in that short time he had doubled the area of the world, as known to the Greeks of his day.

CHAPTER 41

ALEXANDER'S CITY

"Forward, backward, backward, forward, in the immeasurable sea,
Sway'd by vaster ebbs and flows than can be known to you or me."
—TENNYSON.

ALEXANDER THE GREAT was dead, and with his death the mighty empire of the East, that he had founded, crumbled away. But the city, called by his name in Egypt, lived and thrived.

There is a curious story told about the founding of Alexandria. The king had already staked out a piece of ground on which to build his Grecian city, when he had a dream. In his sleep he saw an old grey-headed man, whom he recognised as Homer. Standing over him the Greek poet said—

"An island lies, where loud the billows roar,
Pharos they call it, on the Egyptian shore."

Alexander got up and went off to Pharos at once. He found there a little island, at the mouth of the river Nile, and at once saw how suitable a place this was for a port. Here was a long neck of land stretching, like an isthmus, between large lagoons on one side, and the sea on the other. Hence there was a harbour on the sea side, sheltered by the island of Pharos, and one on the other side, opening to the Nile. The place seemed to be the meeting-point of the whole Nile region, with the Mediterranean world.

The king ordered, that a plan of the city should be marked out; but the soil was black and they had no chalk, so they laid out the lines with flour. Suddenly a number of birds rose up from the lagoons like a black cloud, and pecked up every morsel of the flour. At first the king was troubled; but he soon took heart again when the prophets told him that it was a sign, that the new city would be the feeder of many nations.

So the city rose; it was joined to the island of Pharos, by a causeway of a mile long, and its greatness, as a mart of the world, must have far surpassed the wildest dreams of Alexander. He had opened up new channels of trade, and raised fresh wants and fresh hopes for each country he conquered. In the vast tracts of country through which he had passed, he had founded Greek cities and colonies peopled by Greeks, who taught the Eastern folk something of trade and habits of industry.

Thus new articles of commerce, of which the Western world knew nothing, were brought to light; a cotton tree was discovered, from which paper could be made, shawls were created from the hair of the goats found in Thibet, rice was brought from India, and wine was made from the juice of palms.

In the foundation of Alexandria the king showed he was keenly alive to the value of commerce between Europe and the East; but more important still, he was the first to see, that the command of the sea, is necessary to the possession of land.

So vessels plied up and down the Mediterranean Sea, backwards and forwards, bringing merchandise to Alexandria, trading with Athens, with Carthage, with Syracuse, with Rome, with the East, until the city grew and grew. A wonderful lighthouse, of white marble, was built on the island of Pharos, four hundred feet high, which was reckoned among the seven wonders of the world. Fires were lit on its summit to guide the vessels safely into port; and to-day a modern lighthouse stands on the same spot, flashing out its light far over the dark waters, to guide the great steamers on their way from Europe to India.

Heavy and round were the old ships, that were used for the merchant service in those days. Many a one might be seen in the port of Alexandria with its single sail, its curly prow, and the eye painted on either side to ward off ill-luck. Often enough these ships were painted bright colours,—blue, purple, and red,—and must have looked quaint enough, as they put out to sea in the fine summer weather. They could only sail for certain months in the year.

"For fifty days before the end of the harvest is the tide for sailing," says an old writer; "then you will not wreck your ship, nor will the sea wash down your crew. In that season winds are steady and ocean kind: with mind at rest, launch your ship and stow your freight, but make all speed to return home, and await not till the winter approaches and the terrible South wind stirs the waves and makes the sea cruel."

In the port of Alexandria too, as well as on the seas, might be seen some of the Greek warships known as triremes. They were built with three rows of benches, one above another, on each bench two rowers, so that sometimes there were as many as one hundred and seventy rowers in the ship.

It was all very different in those days to what it is now, when no ship is rowed at sea, save near the coast. Winter and summer, through night and through day, the great steamships of all countries ride the rough seas, carrying cargoes from one land to another.

CHAPTER 42

BACK TO ROME AGAIN

"The Gaul shall come against thee
From the land of snow and night;
Thou shalt give his fair-haired armies
To the raven and the kite."
—MACAULAY.

WE left Rome struggling to assert herself above the neighbouring tribes of Italy. But she had further struggles before her, before she should be free and great—great enough to conquer even Greece herself.

Some hundred years had passed away, since the death of the traitor Coriolanus, and one Camillus was now Dictator.

And now some new foes began to sweep down, from the north, towards Rome. They were known to the Romans, as the Gauls, a fierce and savage people, who loved fighting. They were tall, strong men with fair hair, unlike the dark Romans. They dressed in bright colours, with gold collars round their necks, carrying round shields and huge broadswords.

Over the Alps came these savage warriors, on and on towards Rome herself. No one had ever seen the like of them before, and the Romans grew very much alarmed, when they heard the Gauls shouting out their war-songs and clashing their arms like barbarians.

A fight took place near Rome in which the Gauls were victorious, and Brennus, the King of the Gauls, led his rough army into Rome. To their surprise they found the city empty. Terror had seized the Romans. They had no hope of defending their city, so they made their way, with their women and children, to the Capitol, a steep rocky hill, defended with strong walls, the great national temple of old Rome, where they hoped to be safe.

The city itself was empty save for a few infirm and sick people, a little garrison, and eighty old senators, who determined to sit still in the Forum and await the foe. They were too old to flee; they thought if they sacrificed themselves to the gods, the city would be saved. They dressed themselves in their splendid robes of state, and sat down in a row, with their ivory staves in their hands, on their ivory chairs, to await what they knew must be their end.

The savage Gauls burst into Rome. When they came to the Forum they stood amazed, at the sight of the eighty grand old men, sitting calm and still in their chairs. One of the Gauls put out his hand to touch one of the long white beards, but the old man resented it and struck the rude soldier with his ivory staff. At this, the Gaul instantly drew his sword, and killed the old Roman. Then the slaughter began. The Gauls killed the old men, plundered their houses, and then attacked the Capitol.

The Romans let them come half-way up, and then hurled them down the steep rocks. As they could not take the Capitol by force, the Gauls now laid siege to it. Time went on and the brave Romans were nearly starved, shut up in the lofty Capitol and surrounded by their enemies. At last a Roman made his way through the Gauls at night, climbed the steep rock to the Capitol, and told the weary garrison, that Camillus was coming with an army to rescue them. Then he slid down the rock and made his way back safely. But the broken twigs and torn ivy, showed the Gauls, that the Capitol had been scaled. What man had done, man could do.

So King Brennus sent up some of his men by night in twos; they crept up silently, but just as they came to the top, some geese began to cackle and scream, and a Roman ran out, to see what was the matter. There he saw a tall Gaul standing on the wall, at the top of the rock. Rushing at him, he struck him such a blow, that knocked him right off the wall, and down the rocks, and no other Gauls dared to climb up.

But in the end the Romans won; for Camillus arrived on the scene, defeated the Gauls, took their camp, and not a man was left to carry back the news to their own country.

So Rome shook herself free once more, and Camillus was always known, as the second founder of Rome, for he had saved his city from the Gauls.

CHAPTER 43

A GREAT CONFLICT

"The Greek shall come against thee,
The conqueror of the East."
—MACAULAY.

As the years rolled on, the power of Rome grew greater. While King Alexander was conquering in the East, she was subduing tribe after tribe in Italy. But still on the sea-coasts of the south, there were many towns built by the Greeks, who had sailed over the sea and settled there. Now there was a quarrel between the Greeks of a city called Tarentum and the Romans. The people of Tarentum, unable to defend themselves against so powerful a foe as Rome, sent to the mother country for help.

One winter's night, in the midst of a boisterous storm, the waves of the Mediterranean washed upon the shores of Southern Italy a brave man. He was more dead than alive, for he had thrown himself overboard, from the prow of a royal Greek ship, and had been sorely buffeted by the wind and the waves. They had no respect for a royal crown; they knew not, that he was a king ruling over a strong people, and that he had left his kingdom, with thousands of archers and footmen and knights, together with a quantity of huge elephants.

It was no less a person than Pyrrhus, king of a part of Greece. He had taken Alexander the Great as his model, and already conquered Macedonia. Hearing that his fellow-countrymen were in trouble with the Romans, he made up his mind to go and help them. And this is how he came to be voyaging in haste to Italy, and how he came to be shipwrecked on this winter's night.

Before he started one of his counsellors asked the king, what he should do, if he beat the Romans, who were reputed great warriors.

"The Romans overcome," answered the king, "no city would dare to oppose me, and I should be master of all Italy."

"And Italy conquered, what next?" asked the counsellor.

"Sicily next holds out her arms to receive us," he answered. "She is a wealthy and populous island and easy to be gained."

"And what next?" asked the counsellor again.

"There is Africa and Carthage," said the king. "Then I should be able to master all Greece."

"And then?" continued the counsellor.

"Then I would live at ease, eat and drink all day, and enjoy pleasant conversation."

"And what hinders you now, from taking the ease, that you are planning to take, after so much risk and bloodshed?"

Pyrrhus could not answer this question. His ambition to be like the great king, Alexander, led him on.

Once landed on the shores of Italy, he marched to Tarentum. There he found an idle colony of Greeks, given up to pleasure. Pyrrhus soon shut up their places of amusement and trained the young men as soldiers.

A great battle took place. The Romans could easily see, which was the Greek king, by his splendid armour and scarlet mantle. So marked was he, that presently he gave his glittering arms and mantle to one of his officers, knowing well that if he were killed, the Romans would easily win the day. The battle was long and fierce. The officer wearing the king's scarlet mantle was suddenly killed. The Greeks thought that Pyrrhus was killed and began to retreat. But the king threw off his helmet, rode bareheaded through the ranks, and rallied his soldiers.

Then he ordered a charge of the elephants. The Romans had never seen these monsters in battle before; their horses were terrified in the same way that Alexander's had been in the battle with Porus, the Indian king, and they turned and fled in confusion. When Pyrrhus looked at the field of battle, and saw the Romans lying dead, with their faces to the foe, he cried out, "Oh, how easy would it be for me to conquer the world, if I had the Romans for my soldiers."

The following year another great battle was fought between the Greeks and Romans; but the Romans no longer feared the elephants in battle, for they had learnt that these animals are afraid of fire. They got ready bundles of sticks, dipped in pitch, which they lighted and threw among them. The elephants were terrified of the fire; they turned round and ran wildly about among the Greeks, trampling down a great many and killing more. So the battle ended; Pyrrhus fled at once from Italy and sailed away to Greece.

And Rome gloried in her victory. The houses were decked with flowers; every window was filled with faces; the streets were crowded to see the great procession wending its way to the Capitol. First in the procession, walked the senators; then, guarded by Roman soldiers, came the spoils taken from the Greeks, piled high on waggons—beautiful pictures and statues, robes and armour, were there; together with all sorts of things, made by the skilful Greeks and never even seen by the simple Romans. Here, too, were the great elephants, seen for the first time in the streets of Rome.

There were soldiers of Greece too, the finest foot-soldiers in the world; and at last came a triumphal car, in which sat the Roman general, who had gained this victory for his country. He wore a splendid mantle, embroidered with gold, he was crowned with a laurel wreath, and in his right hand, he carried a laurel bough. Behind him rode his officers, with laurel garlands, twisted round their spears, singing the praises of their successful general.

So the Romans mounted the steep way to the Capitol, to give thanks to their god, for the victory and deliverance from the Greeks.

CHAPTER 44

THE ROMAN FLEET

"Over the seas our galleys went,
With cleaving prows in order brave,
To a speeding wind and a bounding wave—
A gallant armament."
—R. BROWNING.

HARDLY had Pyrrhus turned his back for the last time on Italy, when the first note of war, sounded between the Romans, and the men of Carthage. It came from that fair island—the foot of Italy, the Cyclops of the old Argonauts—Sicily. As Pyrrhus disappeared from the Western world he had cried, with his last breath, half in pity, half in envy, "How fair a battlefield are we leaving to the Romans and Carthaginians!"

The battlefield for the next hundred years was to be Sicily. Sooner or later, all knew that the struggle must come—the struggle for power between these two great nations. It was not a struggle for Sicily only, it was a contest for the sea— for possession of the blue Mediterranean, that washed the shores of Italy, that carried the ships of

Carthage into every known port in Europe and North Africa.

Theirs was the greatest of all islands, the island of Sardinia; theirs the tiny Elba, with its wondrous supply of metals; theirs Malta, the outpost. From the Altar of the Philenæ on the one side to the Pillars of Hercules, on the other, stretched the country of the Carthaginians, the richest land of the ancient world. No wonder, then, they viewed the growing power of Rome with distrust; no wonder they prepared for the struggle, which they knew must come.

The Romans were not so well prepared. Up to this time all their fighting had been by land, they knew nothing of the sea. Great as soldiers, they had not the enterprise, that had prompted the sailors of Tyre and of Carthage, to enlarge the bounds of the world, and to guide their home-made ships into unknown seas.

To the Romans, as to the Egyptians, the great salt ocean, was an object of terror. But now the time had come, when the Romans must have a navy. They had some of the old triremes, such as the Greeks used; but they knew that the Carthaginians had newer and better ships at sea, than these old triremes, with their three banks of oars. One day, says an old story, a large ship from Carthage was washed ashore on the coast of Italy. It was a war vessel with sails and five banks of oars. The Romans set to work to copy it. Within sixty days, a growing wood was cut down and built into a fleet of a hundred ships on the new model. While the hundred ships were building, it is said, a large number of Roman landsmen were trained to row on dry land, and in two months the new fleet put to sea.

Never did ships sail under greater difficulties. But with admirable pluck, the sea-sick landsmen pulled their oars, heedless of the starting timbers, of the new unseasoned wood of their vessels. And forth into the Mediterranean, went the Romans against their new foes.

But the skill in naval warfare, which had taken the Carthaginians years and years to learn, could not be mastered by the men of Rome in a day. They devised a new method of naval fighting, by which they could board the enemy's ships and fight hand to hand. It was a clumsy idea, but they won their first sea-fight with the foe. They put up a strong mast, on the front of each ship, to which they lashed a kind of drawbridge, with a sharp spike of strong iron at the end, not unlike the long bill of a raven. When the enemy's ship drew near, they would let this heavy drawbridge fall with a crash, on to the deck of the attacking ship. The iron beak would pierce the planking, and in a few moments the Roman sailors would be on board the Carthaginian ships locked in a hand-to-hand battle.

Off the coast of Sicily the Carthaginians met the clumsy Roman fleet. They bore down upon it, laughing at the strange appearance of the vessels with uncouth masts, and wondering what was hanging on to those masts. Confidently thirty ships of Carthage advanced their decks cleared for action.

What was their surprise then, to find themselves suddenly imprisoned, by the iron beaks, which had excited their contempt, but a short time before. Round swung the fatal raven, pinning the ships together, while the Romans were leaping on to their decks, and fighting them hand to hand. After fifty of their ships of war had been destroyed in this way, the remainder refused to fight any more, and the Romans returned home, having won their first naval victory over the greatest naval Power, the world had yet seen.

A pillar was put up in the Forum, at Rome, adorned with the brazen beaks of the Carthaginian ships, which the clumsy skill of the Romans had enabled them to capture.

CHAPTER 45

HANNIBAL'S VOW

"Roll on, thou deep and dark blue Ocean—roll;
Ten thousand fleets sweep over thee in vain."
—BYRON.

FIFTEEN years passed away and Rome and Carthage were still fighting for the mastery of the sea. Since the victory of Mylæ, the Roman fleet had been beaten more than once, by the Carthaginians—these weather-wise masters of the sea.

It was about this time that one great man, called Hamilcar, appeared on the scene at Carthage, and to him the Carthaginians entrusted the command of their army. The war dragged on listlessly, for another eight years, and then Hamilcar made peace with the Romans. He consented, on behalf of the Carthaginians, to give up the island of Sicily to Rome; but he had made great plans of his own, by which he hoped that his own country should yet retain the command of the Mediterranean. Hamilcar had patience and genius, he loved his country with true patriotism, he hated the very name of Rome, and, moreover, he had an infant

181

son, whom he was bringing up in the same spirit. This was the boy Hannibal, who was to become one of the greatest men, the world had ever seen.

And all the while, this Hamilcar was dreaming of an empire in Spain—an empire rich, powerful, mighty, which should more than make up to the Carthaginians for the loss of Sicily. Accompanied by the fleet, he made his way slowly along the north African coast, reached Gibraltar, and set foot for the first time in Spain. With him was his little nine-year-old son Hannibal.

There is an old story, which tells us, that Hamilcar was sacrificing to the god of his country, before starting forth to Spain, when he suddenly bade his servants withdraw, while he asked the little Hannibal, if he would like to go with him to the wars. The boy eagerly said "Yes."

"Then," said his father, "lay your hand on the sacrifice and swear eternal hatred to Rome."

The little boy did as he was told, and right faithfully through his whole life did he keep his oath.

It was indeed into a land of promise that Hamilcar and his little son now passed; for the next nine years he worked industriously. Under him the gold and silver mines of Spain yielded double their old value, which enabled him to collect a Spanish army. He worked to carry out his magnificent schemes, until he died a soldier's death in battle, leaving his son-in-law, Hasdrubal, and his young son

Hannibal to fulfil his dying heritage, of eternal hatred of Rome.

Hasdrubal enlarged the empire he had founded in Spain, giving it a capital in New Carthage. It was an excellent harbour, and soon rose to rival its namesake on the opposite coast. When Hasdrubal died some years later, Hannibal, now a man of twenty-nine, was chosen as commander of the Spanish army. He had already distinguished himself by fighting under his father, and he had not forgotten his oath of revenge. He at once began to prepare for war with Rome by taking a town that had formed an alliance with Rome. Then the Romans sent messengers to Hannibal.

"We bring you peace or war," they said. "Take which you please."

"War," was Hannibal's fierce answer. And war it was.

Hannibal retreated into winter quarters at New Carthage and dismissed his Spanish troops to their homes.

"Come back in the early spring," he said, "and I will be your leader in a war, from which, both the glory and the gain will be immense."

So the rival nations prepared for battle. The die was now cast and the arena cleared for the foremost man of his race and his time, to show himself the greatest military genius, that the world had ever seen.

CHAPTER 46

THE ADVENTURES OF HANNIBAL

"Attempt not to acquire that, which may not be retained."
—FOUNDERS OF CARTHAGE.

LEAVING Spain to the care of his younger brother Hasdrubal, Hannibal set out from New Carthage, with his Spanish troops, a number of horses, and thirty-seven elephants—set out to accomplish a feat, which still fills the world with wonder and admiration. Why he did not sail across the sea from New Carthage to Italy, with a fleet, is not known; he preferred to scale the mountain passes, which led him by land into the country he fain would make his own. Over the high Pyrenees, mountains which divide Spain from France, the army started and marched up the valley of the Rhone. Crossing the river at a spot "nearly four days' journey from the sea," they soon found themselves at the foot of the Alps.

The passes of these sharply peaked mountains, which soar high above the snow-line, have always been the gate of traffic, between Italy and the rest of Europe. To-day a railway runs right through one of the passes and through the region of eternal snow.

Hannibal's difficulties now began. The one track over the mountains, was occupied in force by mountaineers, but Hannibal found out that these people always returned to their homes at night. So when darkness fell, he took his most active troops, and climbed up to the place, just left by the mountaineers.

Next morning, the rest of the army followed, winding slowly and painfully up the steep pass. The path was very narrow, and many of the horses and elephants lost their footing, and rolled headlong down the precipices, carrying the baggage with them. The whole army moved forward, descending into a rich valley, where the natives seemed friendly enough.

They now entered the narrow way, leading to the main mountain wall of the Alps; the one barrier, that yet separated Hannibal from the land of his hopes. Here the cliffs rose steeply above them and the torrent foamed angrily below; but they pushed bravely on, till suddenly, stones came thundering down, from the natives, on the heights, and it seemed for a time, as if the whole army must perish. Here, at the "white stone," which is still standing at the foot of the St Bernard Pass, Hannibal stood to arms the whole night through, while his army passed on upwards.

On the ninth day, they reached the top, and a two days' rest was ordered. It was a sorry spot on which to recruit. It was late in October, snow lay thick on the peaks above, and the troops, drawn from burning Africa and sunny Spain, shivered in the keen mountain air. Depression seized them. Their ranks were sadly thinned, and the paths were getting more and more difficult, but the enthusiasm of their leader remained the same. In a few stirring words, he bid them keep up heart. Below their feet lay Italy—the land of their desire. "You are climbing not the walls of Italy only, but of Rome herself," cried Hannibal to his weary men. "After one or two battles we shall have the capital of Italy in our hands. Yonder," he cried, pointing away to the fair horizon, where he saw, in his mind's eye, the goal of all his hopes—"yonder lies Rome."

The spirits of the soldiers rose, and amid falling snow, they began the descent. More dangers awaited them. They had to march over a steep and slippery ice slope, just covered with a thin coating of freshly fallen snow. Men, horses, and elephants slipped and rolled about, now sticking fast in a snowdrift, now falling into a chasm, now preferring death in the snow, to the struggle of going on. At last they reached a spot, where the track was lost and neither man nor beast could pass. Destruction once more stared them in the face. But Hannibal's pluck did not fail him. He set the soldiers to work to make a new road, over which he took the army. And so, at last they descended into the plains of Italy.

Hannibal had succeeded, but the sacrifice was enormous. More than half his men had perished; horses and elephants had died in that dreaded march of over 500 miles, in that month of misery. It was a wonderful feat; but still more wonderful was the fact that he defeated the whole Roman army, not once but twice, with his wayworn men, until there seemed nothing to bar his road, right on to the city of Rome.

The Gauls—those wild enemies of Rome—now joined him, and he led them over the Apennines and into the valley of the Arno. The melting of the snows on the mountains had caused the Arno to overflow, converting the plain into a vast swamp. For four days and nights the army toiled through the water, unable to find a dry spot, either to sit down or sleep. The horses fell in heaps, the Gauls grumbled loudly, Hannibal himself was tortured with inflammation in his eyes. He rode bravely onwards, on the one elephant that had survived, and escaped with only the loss of an eye.

On the shores of a great lake, not far from Rome, he met the Roman army. There was a thick fog, through which the Romans advanced, only to find, as the mist rolled away, that they were advancing into the jaws of death. Their whole army was cut up by Hannibal, and but few returned to carry back the sad tidings to Rome, to destroy the bridges over the Tiber, and prepare for the advance of Hannibal to their capital.

CHAPTER 47

THE END OF CARTHAGE

"Now sleep and silence brood o'er the city."
—GOLDSMITH.

WHEN the news of the disaster reached Rome an anxious crowd gathered in the Forum.

"We have been defeated in a great battle," said the chief magistrate, towards sunset, mounting the orator's platform in the Forum. Day after day the senators sat from sunrise to sunset, preparing now for the worst. But Hannibal did not march on Rome, and the Romans took heart again and prepared another great army to fight the Carthaginian general.

Once more the two armies met, once more the Romans were defeated, and Hannibal stood victorious on the battlefield of Cannæ. To show Carthage how great had been his victory, he sent ten thousand of the gold rings, taken from the fingers of the Roman nobles, slain in this battle.

Hannibal was now at the height of his success. From the day he had set forth over the Pyrenees, he had known no defeat; now, under the spell of his genius, hundreds flocked to his standard.

But while the successful Carthaginian was carrying all before him, a young Roman soldier was making a name for himself, by carrying the war into Spain. Young Scipio managed very cleverly to take New Carthage, the great Carthaginian seaport on the southern coast of Spain, with its mines of gold and silver, its merchant vessels and its fine dockyards,— all of which were a terrible loss to Carthage.

"I see the doom of Carthage," exclaimed Hannibal at last, when his brother's head was brought to him after a defeat by the Romans.

Still he kept his army in Italy, waiting for the opportunity that should give him the object of his life—Rome. But the opportunity never came. Before he had gathered an army strong enough, to march on Italy's capital, he was recalled to his native land to defend Carthage against Scipio.

The scheme of his boyhood and manhood was spoiled, and it is said the great commander could hardly restrain his tears, as the ships bore him from the land, he had failed to conquer—the land in which he had spent fifteen years of his life—across the sea to North Africa. It was thirty-six years since he had left Carthage with his father, thirty-six years since he had laid his small hand, on the sacrifice, and sworn undying hatred to Rome.

One autumn day in the year 202, the two great commanders, Hannibal and Scipio, met for the first and last time in battle. The battle of Zama was to decide for centuries to come, the fate of Rome—it was to make her supreme among the nations of the Old World. The battlefield lay some five days' journey to the south of Carthage, amid the sandy wastes of the North African desert land.

In the forefront of Hannibal's army marched a magnificent array of eighty elephants, but they were terrified at the blare of the trumpets, and fled in confusion right among Scipio's soldiers. He had wisely prepared for this, and the elephants were more cumbrous, than helpful. After a hard fight the Romans won, and Hannibal, the hero of a hundred battles, made his way to Carthage—a defeated man.

With dignity and self respect he accepted his failure; though it must have been bitter to him to bow down to the terms of peace, now offered by Scipio. True, the Carthaginians were to keep their own laws, and their own home; but they were to give up all their prisoners, all their elephants, and all their warships save ten; they were to renounce all claim to the rich islands in the Mediterranean and to their kingdom of Spain, and for the next fifty years they must pay a large sum of money to Rome.

Yet a further humiliation was in store for Hannibal and the Carthaginians. Five hundred ships—the pride and glory of the Phœnician race, ships which had sailed up and down the Mediterranean trading with this port and that—were slowly towed out of the harbour and set on fire by the victorious Romans, in the sight of the fallen Carthaginians.

"And a cry was heard, unfathered of earthly lips,
  What of the ships, O Carthage? Carthage, what of the ships?"

The sight of the flames was terrible to the vanquished people—as terrible as if their very city had been burnt.

"And the smouldering grief of a nation burst with the kindling blaze."

In the days of her prosperity, when a storm at sea destroyed some of her ships, the whole State would go into mourning, and the huge walls of the city would be draped in black. What must their feelings be now, when the whole fleet was blazing under their very eyes, and with it their command of the sea was gone for ever!

So Carthage fell, overcome by her dreams of conquest. She had acquired that she could not retain, she had envied that, she could not possess. And what is left of her to-day? A few scattered piles of stones, some broken columns, and a few old tombs, are the only fragments of her glorious past. Carthage herself, the home of Hannibal, the victor of nations, mother of cities, centre of the world's commerce, lies crumbled in the sand and dust of two thousand years.

CHAPTER 48

THE TRIUMPH OF ROME

" 'Tis Greece, but living Greece no more."
—BYRON.

ROME had conquered Carthage. Where the busy Phœnicians had lived and thriven for five hundred years, Romans now pastured the herds of their distant masters. Roman merchants flocked across the seas to this new Roman province, called now— for the first time in history—Africa.

Flushed with her victories here, she turned her eyes towards Greece—toward the country, which Alexander the Great had made so strong, but which was now crumbling into decay, under one Perseus.

The Romans now chose one of their consuls, the brother-in-law of the dead Scipio, to march against Macedonia. That kingdom once subdued, they knew that Greece would soon fall under their sway.

There is a quaint old story about this brother-in-law of the great Scipio. His name was Paulus, the

Roman word for Paul. He had just been chosen general of the Roman troops, and was coming home when he met his little daughter weeping bitterly.

"What is the matter?" he asked, drawing the child to him.

Throwing her arms round his neck and kissing him, she cried, "O father, do you not know that Perseus is dead?"

Paulus must have wished the news was true, with regard to the enemy, against whom, he was so soon to march; but the little girl was crying over the death of a favourite dog, named Perseus, and her father could only kiss her, saying, "Good fortune, my little daughter, I accept the omen."

So Paulus went off to the wars, and it was not long before the news reached Rome, that he had conquered the Macedonians, and was bringing back Perseus as a prisoner. He sailed up the river Tiber in the king's galley, with its sixteen banks of oars. It was richly adorned with arms captured from the Greeks, with cloths of purple and scarlet. As the vessel was rowed slowly against the stream, the Romans crowded on the shore to meet him. And the Romans decreed a triumph for the conqueror—a triumph, which lasted three days, the like of which had never been seen before. The people erected scaffolds in the Forum and dressed themselves in white.

On the first day two hundred and fifty chariots passed through the streets, with the beautiful statues, pictures, and colossal images, which had been brought from Greece, the home of art and beauty.

On the second day, waggons carried the magnificent armour of the Macedonians, all polished and glittering. There were shields and coats of mail, targets, quivers of arrows, and naked swords all piled up in confusion. After the waggons came three thousand men carrying seven hundred and fifty vessels of silver, while others followed with silver bowls and cups—all of which impressed the Romans very much.

But for the third day, was reserved the greatest triumph of all. Quite early in the morning, the trumpeters sounded, and a number of young Romans appeared, wearing frocks with ornamented borders and leading one hundred and twenty oxen with their horns gilded and adorned with ribbons and garlands, to be sacrificed. Then came all the gold plate, that had been used at the table of the king of rich Macedonia, followed by the chariot of Perseus himself, in which lay his armour and his crown.

A sight followed that drew tears from the eyes of the Roman crowd. The king's three little children were led captives, surrounded by a train of attendants, masters, and teachers, all stretching out their hands to the spectators and entreating pity. Perseus himself followed, clad all in black and "wearing the boots of his country"; he looked like one stunned, through the greatness of his misfortunes. A number of his friends, sobbing with grief, followed.

Then came Paulus himself, seated on a magnificent chariot. He was an old man and worthy to be looked at, in his purple robe interwoven with gold, holding a laurel branch in his right hand. The whole Roman army followed with boughs of laurel in their hands, singing verses and songs of triumph in praise of the deeds of Paulus. And this ended the great procession.

So Greece became subject to the ever-growing power of Rome, and she has never returned to the pinnacle of glory that once made her the chief nation in the Old World.

CHAPTER 49

TWO YOUNG ROMANS

"Great men have been among us."
—WORDSWORTH.

Two men were now pushing their way to the forefront of affairs in Rome—men whose names were to become famous, not only in the history of their own country, but famous in the history of the whole world. Their names were Pompey and Cæsar. They were born within six years of one another, about a hundred years before the birth of Christ, and they were young men still, when they became rivals for Roman power.

Pompey first made his mark. As a child he was very beautiful, and he was ever beloved by the people of Rome for his gentle ways and his kingly manners. He early distinguished himself by fighting, for Rome had still enemies left in both Spain and Africa. On his return from the wars, though still a very young man, he was made consul of Rome.

There is a story told of him at this time, which shows how popular he was. There was an ancient custom in Rome, by which the knights, who had served their time in the wars, led their horses into the market-place, before two officers: they gave an account of their service and received their discharge, every man with honour or disgrace, according to his deserts. The knights were passing thus, before the officers, when Pompey was seen leading his horse into the Forum, wearing the dress of a consul.

"Pompey the Great," said the senior officer, "I demand of you, whether you have served the full time in the laws which is ordered by the Roman law."

"Yes," replied Pompey in a loud voice, "I have served all, and all under myself as general."

On hearing this all the people gave a great shout, and they went on shouting, till the officers rose from their judgment-seat and accompanied the hero to his home, amid the clapping of hands and shouts of joy.

When his term of office was over he was given authority, for three years, over the whole Mediterranean Sea, so that he might crush out the pirates or sea-robbers, who were ruining the trade of that great sea.

Now these sea-robbers were growing very dangerous. They had built for themselves swift-sailing ships, with which to pursue the merchant vessels; they had harbours, towers, and beacons, all round the sea-coast. Their ships had gilded masts, the sails were purple, the oars plated with silver. They were the terror of navigators from the Straits of Gibraltar, to the shores of the Black Sea; they stopped and robbed the ships bringing wheat from Sicily and Alexandria, to feed the Romans, and it was plain that something must be done.

Pompey divided the sea into thirteen parts, and sent officers and men to fight the sea-robbers in each part. Up and down the blue Mediterranean, sailed these ships, chasing the pirates, till in forty days the whole sea was cleared and Pompey was free to undertake some new work, for his country. The great kingdoms of the East were once more on the war-path, and Pompey was now sent to subdue them.

When Pompey next returned to Rome, he was at the height of his glory. He had marched a great Roman army through Syria; he had extended the Roman Empire, as far as the river Euphrates. It was small wonder, then, that Rome accorded him a two days' triumph, which exceeded in magnificence, even the triumph of Paulus. All his great deeds were set forth on bronze tablets which were carried before him. These told how he had founded cities, captured eight hundred ships, one thousand fortresses, and nearly as many towns; he had poured money wholesale into the treasury of Rome, while three hundred captive princes walked before his chariot. He returned triumphant, and dreams of kingship were already in his mind. He had left Rome but four years before, the very idol of the people.

"Knew you not Pompey? Many a time and oft
Have you climbed up to walls and battlements,
To towers and windows, yea, to chimney-tops,
Your infants in your arms, and there have sat
The livelong day with patient expectation
To see great Pompey pass the streets of Rome;
And when you saw his chariot but appear,
Have you not made an universal shout
Till Tiber trembled underneath her banks?"

But now, as he stepped from his chariot after his triumph, Pompey the Great found himself alone; no longer was he surrounded by admirers and flatterers, no longer was he the idol of Rome.

For another favourite had enthroned himself in the hearts of the people. And that was Julius Cæsar—a far greater man than Pompey could ever be, for

"This was the greatest Roman of them all."

CHAPTER 50

JULIUS CÆSAR

"Veni, vidi, vici"—"I came, I saw, I conquered."
—CÆSAR.

LET us take a look at this Cæsar, whose name and deeds are talked of still, though nearly two thousand years have rolled away, since he lived and died in far-off Rome. He was now growing up, in his father's house, a tall handsome youth, with dark piercing eyes, a sallow face, somewhat thick lips, and a high forehead.

As quite a young boy, he must have seen and heard much, about his country. He must have known well, his uncle Marius, who was a great soldier and did much for Rome, till he was exiled in disgrace, by those he had tried to serve. Sulla, the rival of Marius, he knew well too, for had not this powerful Dictator uttered the ominous words—"I charge you to look after this youth with the loose girdle, for in this young Cæsar, there is many a Marius"?

Having incurred Sulla's wrath, Cæsar joined the Roman army and left Italy. He distinguished himself in the field, both in Asia and in Spain, and returned to Rome to find the work of his life.

He was now a marked man; he had spoken in the Senate; he had been consul; he had pleaded in favour of the appointment of Pompey to his high commands, and Pompey had married his daughter Julia. It was to him the Romans now looked, to rid them of a great danger, which threatened them in the north. Gaul and Germany were once more in a state of great unrest, and might at any time let loose their wild armies, in the plains of North Italy. Cæsar was forty-two, when he left Rome to take up his military command in Gaul.

As a younger man, reading the life of Alexander the Great, he had burst into tears, and on being asked the reason he had answered, "Do you not think I have just cause to weep, when I consider that Alexander at my age, had conquered so many nations, and I have all this time done nothing that is memorable?"

He was yet to make himself a name as great, if not greater, than his hero. To subdue these restless tribes beyond the Alps—the country we now know as Switzerland, France, and Germany—was Cæsar's object in life, and to establish the power of Rome over them.

New countries, undreamt of by Rome, were now discovered, by the ever-advancing army under Cæsar. Across the great German Rhine, and over the French Seine, he passed, conquering and subduing the fierce tribes, which fell back before the trained

Roman legions, under their great commander. Arrived at the north of France, Cæsar looked across the Channel from Calais and saw the white cliffs on the English coast.

No one could tell him anything of that country, so, one calm evening, he sailed from the coast of France, and morning found him off the coast of Dover. The white cliffs were lined with painted warriors, waving lances, and ready to hurl large stones into Cæsar's ship, if he attempted to land. Calling his officers round him, while his fleet collected, he ordered them to move along the coast with the tide. The Britons followed by the cliffs, scrambling along with their cars and horses. It was evident they meant to oppose any landing.

Cæsar anchored near the shore, but the water was up to the shoulders of the Roman soldiers. Then an officer sprang into the sea, waving the standard of the Roman eagle, and cried to his men to follow. With a great cheer the men sprang overboard. The Britons rode their horses into the waves and for a time stopped their progress, but the Romans managed to land and the Britons galloped away. Some sharp fighting took place on land, but the wild tribes were no match for the Romans.

It was now nine years since Cæsar had left Rome. Now he had made a name indeed for himself. He was returning to lay at his country's feet, a province larger than Spain, new lands of which the Romans had never heard, warriors devoted to himself, and a detailed history of all his doings. His countrymen had watched his career steadily. The Senate had listened to every story of his marches and battles, his perils and victories, as they were recited one by one.

"Cæsar has not only repulsed the Gauls, he has conquered them," cried Cicero, one of the greatest of Romans. "The Alps were once the barrier between Italy and the barbarians; the gods placed them there, for that very purpose—to shelter Rome in the weakness of her infancy. Now let them sink and welcome; from the Alps to the ocean she has no enemy to fear."

But there was one man in Rome who watched Cæsar's growing power with dismay. It was Pompey, now consul of Rome. He dreaded the return and triumph of this great conqueror, whose name was on every lip, of whose genius none could speak too highly. The return of Cæsar would mean the fall of Pompey, for Cæsar had been promised the consulship. The state of Rome was very corrupt at this time. Men were afraid of offending Pompey; they were yet more afraid of Cæsar, with his legions in the north. Day by day matters grew worse; was it to be peace or war?

The answer was not long in coming. It was war.

CHAPTER 51

THE FLIGHT OF POMPEY

"Oh you hard hearts, you cruel men of Rome,
　Knew you not Pompey?"
　　　　　　　　　—SHAKSPERE.

CÆSAR now assembled his soldiers on the banks of
the river Rubicon, which divided Italy from Gaul.
The Romans still thought his heart might fail or his
troops desert him. But neither of these things
happened. True, it is said, that for a moment, the
great conqueror paused.

Suddenly dismayed by the greatness of his
undertaking, he asked himself, was he right to bring
so much trouble on his countrymen? The destinies
of the Roman nation hung on his decision. Then, as
if acting on some sudden impulse, he cried, "The die
is cast." So saying he urged his charger through the
stream. The Rubicon was crossed. He was on his
way to Rome. There could be no turning back now.

The news reached Rome. Cæsar's charger had
been seen on the Apennine hills. He was coming at
last. Pompey did not hesitate. In flight lay his only
safety. Up rose consuls and senators, and leaving

"Cæsar paused on the banks of the Rubicon."

their wives and children to their fate, they fled for their lives, with Pompey, out of Rome. They played the part of cowards, and in the old Roman days, men would not have deserted their city like this.

"It is all panic and blunder," cried Cicero; "the flight of the Senate, the departure of the magistrates, the closing of the treasury, will not stop Cæsar—I am broken-hearted."

Pompey could not raise an army by land, but the sea was his. His was the East with all its treasures, his the fleets of the Mediterranean. Cæsar might win for the moment, but Pompey had the naval power to bring against Italy.

So Cæsar entered Rome in peace. He soon left it again for Spain, where he went to prepare an army and a fleet to fight against Pompey.

"I go," he said to the Romans—"I go to engage an army without a general: I shall return, to attack a general, without an army."

The Romans at once made him Dictator, and he set out for his chase after Pompey. Pompey was in Greece preparing for his great invasion of Italy. It was early in January, just a year since he had crossed the Rubicon, that Cæsar sailed from Brindisi for Greece. Pompey's admiral, from the heights of Corfu, saw his ship. He had let Cæsar pass, but he would not let his soldiers and ships pass in the same way. So Cæsar waited on one side of the Adriatic and his ships and troops on the other. The months passed on and Cæsar watched in vain for the sails of his ships.

There is an old story that says he at last made up his mind to row over to Brindisi and see what had happened. He hired a boat of twelve oars, disguised himself as a slave, crept on board in the night-time, and lay down at the bottom of the boat. It was very rough and the waves were dashing very high on the Greek coast, so high, indeed, as to render the crossing very dangerous. The master of the boat ordered the rowers to turn back. Then the disguised slave arose.

"Go forward, my friend," shouted the great Cæsar, above the roar of wave and wind. "Fear nothing, you carry Cæsar and his fortunes."

The rivals for Roman power met at last, in Greece, and Pompey was defeated once and for ever by Cæsar. Pompey's fall was complete. He escaped secretly on foot to the coast, and getting on board a merchant vessel, sailed to Mitylene, where his wife and son were waiting. His wife received the news with tears, and sinking into Pompey's arms, she cried, "Ah that I should see you reduced to one poor vessel, who were wont to sail in these seas with a fleet of five hundred ships!"

Putting his wife and son on board, Pompey now sailed down the coast of Asia Minor, then across to Cyprus, and on to Egypt. Egypt was under Roman influence, though not exactly a Roman province, and here the fugitive might gain protection.

The country was under a boy king, called Ptolemy, and his sister Cleopatra. Pompey anchored at sea and sent to the young king for permission to land. He was invited to come ashore, and saying good-bye to his wife, he stepped into the boat sent for him. As he stepped ashore, he was treacherously murdered, his head cut off, and his body thrown back into the sea. A devoted slave whom Pompey had set free, watched for the body to be washed on shore; then he wrapped it in his shirt and buried it in the sand, and so the last rites were performed for one, who but a short time since, was second to none in Rome.

Meanwhile Cæsar had been following his fallen foe. Hearing that he had sailed for Egypt, he took ship and landed at Alexandria, to be received by the news of Pompey's death. Hoping to please him, the head of his rival was brought him. From it, he turned in horror and burst into tears, for Pompey had once been his friend.

CHAPTER 52

THE DEATH OF CÆSAR

"The last of all the Romans, fare thee well."
—SHAKSPERE.

AFTER a three months' stay in Egypt, during which time, he made friends with Cleopatra, Cæsar returned to Rome. He had been made Dictator a second time, and was to hold the post for ten years. A thanksgiving of forty days was decreed, temples and statues were raised in his honour, a golden chair was placed in the Senate for him to sit in. He was called the "Father of his country," a name that Cicero had already borne, and four triumphs were celebrated in his honour.

In return Cæsar feasted the Roman people at twenty-two thousand tables, and entertained them at combats of wild animals and gladiators, beneath awnings of the richest silks. For Pompey had built a splendid theatre in Rome, in which lions and elephants, and men known as gladiators, who fought with swords, for the amusement of the people, engaged in combat before crowds of delighted spectators; for the Romans thought the shedding of blood was pleasing to their gods.

But Cæsar did more than this. He made new Roman laws, he tried to bridge over the terrible inequality, between the very rich and the very poor, he added hugely to the number of senators, he arranged the foreign provinces, and he rearranged the calendar. This was a very important piece of work. Up to this time the year had been made to consist of three hundred and fifty-five days; but as that did not exactly fit in, with the revolution of the earth round the sun, an extra month, had to be added at intervals. This made great confusion, and festivals for the harvest and vintage came three months before there was any corn or grapes.

The Julian calendar, as it was called, made the year to consist of three hundred and sixty-five days and six hours; which arrangement lasted for one thousand six hundred years after the death of Cæsar.

So Cæsar became undisputed master of this mighty empire of Rome. He had shown himself to be, not only one of the greatest conquerors, the world had ever seen, but one of the greatest statesmen. He governed Rome, as a king, in all but name. It was reported in the city, that he wished to be called king. Did he not dress in royal purple robes, had he not given himself all the airs of kingship?

One morning some one placed a crown of laurels, upon the head of his statue, which stood in the Forum. It was done publicly, in the midst of a vast crowd, in Cæsar's presence. The wreath was torn down. A few days later, as he was riding through the streets of Rome, he was saluted by the mob as "king." A stifled murmur of disapproval ran through the crowd.

"I am no king, but Cæsar," cried the Roman Dictator hastily.

Yet again the prize of kingship seemed within reach. Cæsar was in his golden chair, dressed in purple, and wearing a wreath of bay wrought in gold, presented by the senators. He was presiding over a popular festival, when suddenly the chief performer approached Cæsar, and drawing a small crown from his girdle he placed it on Cæsar's head, saying, "The people give you this, by my hand."

As Cæsar took off the crown, a loud burst of applause broke from the people.

"I am not king," he said in a loud voice; "the only king of the Romans is Jupiter." Saying which, he ordered the crown to be carried, to the temple of Jupiter, in the Capitol.

The question of kingship was over, but there was a spirit of unrest and distrust abroad in Rome. Men hated this supreme power; they thought Cæsar was a tyrant, and they wished to see Rome free. Cæsar knew there was danger, but he went daily to the Senate, unarmed, and without a guard.

"It is better to suffer death once, than always to live in fear of it," he had replied loftily to those who urged care.

Cicero—the foremost orator of his day—did not agree with such rashness, on the part of one, whose life was yet so precious to Rome.

"Be you watchful," he urged in a brilliant speech in the Senate, where Cæsar was sitting, but a few weeks before his murder. "All our lives are bound up in yours. With sorrow I have heard you say that you have lived long enough. For your country, you have not. Put away, I beseech you, this contempt of death. Be not wise at our expense. Your work is unfinished. It remains for you to rebuild the constitution. Live till this is done. Live till you see your country at peace. Your life shall continue fresh in the memory of ages to come: men will read with wonder of empire and provinces, of the Rhine, the ocean, and the Nile, of battles without number, of amazing victories, of countless monuments and triumphs; but unless this State be wisely established, your name will not live. Therefore, we beseech you, to watch over your own safety."

But Cæsar heeded not, and a secret plot, to kill him, went forward. An important meeting of the Senate had been called for the 15th of March. The day was known in ancient Rome, as the Ides—*i.e.*, the middle day of the month. This was the day fixed for the murder of Cæsar. He had been warned by a soothsayer, that this should happen, and it is said he was restless and nervous, when the morning came. Unarmed, however, he shook off his uneasiness; he crossed the hall of his palace on the way to the senate-house. As he did so, his own statue fell and

213

broke in pieces on the stones. Outside the senate-house, he met the soothsayer, who had warned him.

"The Ides of March are come," said Cæsar, laughing.

"Yes," answered the soothsayer in a low voice, "but they are not gone."

Cæsar entered the senate-house of Rome for the last time. The senators rose to do him honour, as he took his seat, in the golden chair. Men gathered round him. He knew them all. There was not one, who did not owe him gratitude. He had no suspicions.

Suddenly some one stabbed him in the throat. He started from his chair with a cry. He was surrounded by swords and gleaming steel. For a moment he tried to defend himself. Then seeing Brutus, his friend, with raised sword, he drew his cloak over his face, "And thou too, Brutus?" He uttered the words with his last breath as he fell dead at the foot of Pompey's statue, beside his golden chair.

The Senate rose in confusion and rushed out to proclaim to the Romans, that the tyrant was dead, and Rome was free, while the body of the great Cæsar lay alone in the senate-house, where but a few weeks ago, Cicero had told him, that every senator would die, before harm should reach him.

"We have killed the king," cried Cicero in bitterness of heart, "but the kingdom is with us still.

We have taken away the tyrant, but the tyranny still lives."

The great Roman Republic was ended. It had narrowly escaped being a kingdom. It was now to be an empire under an emperor—an empire so vast and so important that the history of the world henceforth became the history of Rome.

CHAPTER 53

THE EMPIRE OF ROME

"Comes the Last Age, of which the Sibyl sang—
A new-born cycle of the rolling years:
Justice returns to earth."

—VIRGIL.

IT was, indeed, a dangerous Rome, to which young Cæsar, now came to claim his birthright; but he soon showed his countrymen, that he was a worthy successor, of his great uncle. Stories were told of him, as an infant, that showed he was marked out for greatness, according to the early ideas of the Romans.

When he was a small baby he was laid in his cradle by his nurse. The next day he was missing and nowhere to be found. They sought for him long, and then found him on a high tower, commanding a view of the sea, lying with his face to the rising sun. When he first began to speak, a story says, that he commanded some troublesome croaking frogs, to be silent, and the frogs have never croaked there since that day.

It was not long, before the Romans made Cæsar's young heir consul, while Mark Antony, who had grasped at power, on the death of the man he had called his friend, was declared to be an enemy of the State. The murderers of Julius Cæsar had, in their turn, been murdered, amongst them the aged Cicero; but Rome was still unsettled, Rome was still dangerous.

"Cleopatra sailed up the river in a gilded vessel, with purple sails and silver oars."

At last Mark Antony fled to raise an army against the young Cæsar. He had schemes of conquering the East and making Alexandria the capital of the world; but instead of this, he became captivated by the beautiful Queen of Egypt, for whom Julius Cæsar had fought before. He had met her in Rome, when she had stayed with Cæsar. Now he met her again at Tarsus, and at once fell captive to her charms and her wit.

Cleopatra sailed up the river, in a gilded vessel, with purple sails and silver oars, to the music of flutes and reed pipes. She lay under an awning spangled with gold, surrounded by her beautiful slaves. Mark Antony soon loved her. He spent all his time with her, he laid aside his Roman dress and his Roman manners to adopt those of Egypt.

Ugly rumours about him, reached Rome, and Cæsar determined to put an end, to this growing power, beyond the seas. He mustered a fleet and army and met the fleet of Antony and Cleopatra off the southern coast of Greece. For some days a rough sea prevented any battle, but when the battle began, it was very unequal. The huge bulks of the Eastern ships were ill adapted for advance or retreat. They were no match for the skilfully managed triremes of the Romans, and while they rolled heavily on the waters, up went the sail of Cleopatra's galley, and, followed by sixty Egyptian ships and the despairing Antony, she fled across the sea to Alexandria. Thither Cæsar followed, by way of Asia and Syria. All the princes of Asia bowed down to him, and Herod, King of Judea, made friends with the conqueror. He arrived at Alexandria, to hear the news, that Antony had killed himself, and that the queen, Cleopatra, had shut herself up in a strong tower.

Once, and once only, Cæsar saw her; she tried to excite his pity, but failed. She discovered that he intended to have her taken to Rome, to take part in his triumph. The humiliation was more than she could bear. The next day she was found lying on her couch, in her royal robes, dead. Her two maids were dying on either side.

"Is this well?" asked the man, who found her.

"It is well for the daughter of kings," answered the dying maid.

And so Egypt became a Roman province.

Cæsar went back to Rome, triumphant. The death of Antony put an end to the fierce struggles, that had torn Rome, for the ten years, following the death of Julius Cæsar. It seemed, as if the great empire of Rome, might have rest for a time now, under the man, who had already done so much. He now occupied not only the highest place in the city and the highest place in the State, but he was chief of the army.

The man who rules an empire and commands the army of that empire is called an emperor; so Cæsar was now an emperor. He also took the name of Augustus, a word applied to things most noble, most dignified, most high. From this time, therefore, we must call him Cæsar Augustus.

Well and wisely did Augustus rule the Roman people. He lived simply amongst them, he dressed as a plain citizen, he joined in the life of the people. His house was unadorned, his meals were taken in haste and were not luxurious. To his Court and to his person he drew the greatest poets and writers of his age. In his reign Virgil, tall, dark, and shy, might have been seen walking about the streets of Rome, while Horace, who had fought for his country in days gone by, was poet-laureate to the emperor. Lesser singers lived too, in these days of prosperity, ever praising the man, who had restored law and order to Rome, the man who had won peace for their great empire—even Cæsar Augustus, the first Emperor of the Roman Empire.

CHAPTER 54

PAX ROMANA

"And it came to pass in those days, that there went out a decree from Cæsar Augustus, that all the world should be taxed. . . . And all went to be taxed, every one into his own city."

—ST LUKE ii.

So there was peace from end to end of the great Roman Empire under Cæsar Augustus. From the great Atlantic Ocean, that washes the western coasts of France and Spain, to the river Euphrates, crossed by Abraham nearly two thousand years before, there was peace. From the German Rhine, to the burning African deserts, there was peace too. Greece, Asia Minor, Egypt—all were quietly resting under the mighty sway of Rome, under the wise rule of the Emperor Cæsar Augustus.

It was time to make a regular division of this great empire, to divide it into provinces, to prepare for a census or numbering of the people. In order to carry out this plan, each family had to go to their own home, however far away that home might be. Herod had made known this command from Rome, and the whole country of Judæa was astir.

221

Living away in distant Nazareth, some eighty miles, from his native town, was one Joseph. He too must journey across the country to obey the command of Cæsar Augustus. Taking his wife Mary, he started off on the eighty-mile journey. The story is familiar to every child.

When Joseph and Mary reached Bethlehem, after a long and weary climb to the hill-city, the town was full of strangers, and there was no room for them in the inn; so they had to be satisfied with sleeping in a manger. And in this manger at Bethlehem, Jesus Christ was born.

The event made no stir, in the great world beyond quiet Judæa. Cæsar Augustus continued to reign over the Roman Empire, ships sailed to and fro over the blue waters of the Mediterranean Sea, men bought and sold as usual, and the news of Mary's little Son was not known outside the country of the East.

But, though as yet unknown to the world at large, the event was one which was destined to throw over the history of the great world the widest, deepest, mightiest influence, that has ever been known.

The birth of Christ passed by unnoticed. His death, thirty years later, was of world-wide interest. The love of Him, has lasted true, throughout two thousand years, and to-day men are ready to live, ready to die, for that love.

TEACHER'S APPENDIX

IT will be noted that the Bible chronology has been used in this book, and that any mention of Egyptian chronology has been purposely omitted, for the reason that it is a subject under deep discussion, and that no satisfactory conclusion has yet been arrived at. See article on Chronology in 'Bible Treasury.'

A few books are here suggested as a help to this period—from the days of Abraham to the Birth of Christ.

Chap.

1-15. *The Illustrated Bible Treasury* in Nelson's Bible.

The Story of Extinct Civilisations of the East. Anderson.

Egypt, Phœnicia, Carthage. The Story of the Nations Series. Illust.

Dwellers on the Nile. Budge. By-Paths of Bible Knowledge. Illust.

Babylonian Life and History. Budge. By-Paths of Bible Knowledge. Illust.

16 and onwards. *Primer on Greece.* Fyffe.

Smith's Smaller *History of Greece.*

Primer on Europe. Freeman.

16. *The Heroes.* Kingsley. Temple Classics.

17. *Iliad.* Homer. Blackwoods' Ancient Classics.

Stories from Homer. Church. Illust.

Æneid. Virgil. Blackwoods' Ancient Classics.

Stories from Virgil. Church. Illust.

18. *Odyssey.* Homer. Blackwoods' Ancient Classics.

The Odyssey. Butcher & Lang. Illust.

24-28. *Greeks and Persians.* Cox. Epochs of Ancient History.

31,32. *Athenian Empire.* Cos. Epochs of Ancient History.

Life of Pericles. Plutarch. Cassell's National Library, No. 50

Greece in the Age of Pericles. Grant.

33. *The Trial and Death of Socrates.* Transl. by Church.

34 and onwards. *Early Rome.* Epochs of Ancient History.

Smith's Smaller *History of Rome.*

Rome. Gilman. Story of the Nations.

36. *Horatius.* Macaulay's Lays of Ancient Rome. Masterpiece Library.

37. *Coriolanus.* Shakspere. Cassell's National Library.

   Coriolanus. Plutarch's Lives. Cassell's National Library, No. 25

38. *Alexander the Great.* Plutarch. Cassell's National Library, No. 9

   Alexander the Great. Story of the Nations.

45. *Carthage.* Story of the Nations.

   Hannibal. Heroes of the Nations.

   Rome and Carthage. Epochs of Ancient History.

50. *Julius Cæsar.* Heroes of the Nations.

   Julius Cæsar. Plutarch. Cassell's National Library, No. 9

   Julius Cæsar. Shakspere. Cassell's National Library.

   Julius Cæsar. A Study by Froude.

CPSIA information can be obtained at www.ICGtesting.com
Printed in the USA
BVOW022356011012

301735BV00001B/59/A

9 781599 150130